# wonder

# wonder

## advent meditations on the miracle of christmas

## David Daniels

**CENTRAL**PRESS

Ministry Resources from
Central Bible Church

Published by Central Press
Central Bible Church
8001 Anderson Boulevard
Fort Worth, Texas 76120
www.wearecentral.org

First Printing 2021

Unless otherwise indicated, Scripture is taken from the Holy Bible, *New International Version*®, Copyright © 1984, 2001, 2010 by Biblica, Inc.™

*To our children and their children:*
*Grant, Laine, Pearson, Jenna,*
*June and Otto*

*As you discover Jesus each day,*
*may you grow more and more*
*in your wonder of the Savior.*

# CONTENTS
# WHAT TO WONDER

The whole earth is filled
with awe at your wonders;
where morning dawns,
where evening fades,
you call forth songs of joy.

—Psalm 65:8

# Introduction
# THE MOST WONDERFUL TIME?

In 2020, most people found themselves in a dark, difficult place. An upcoming election fueled a continuous and contentious news cycle of political rhetoric and mudslinging. A worldwide pandemic fostered fear and uncertainty as people were forced into quarantine, away from their relationships and recreational outlets. With businesses shut down, many people found themselves out of work, suddenly unable to pay for housing, utilities, medical care and other basic needs. Millions of Americans turned to food banks for the first time, while food producers struggled to keep supply lines open across the country. Students and teachers pivoted to online learning, with children feeling the loss of their own educational and social development. Medical professionals struggled to keep up with rising COVID cases, made worse by battles over serious concerns and religious liberties. Episodes of violence—against people of color and in response to racial injustice—set the United States on edge. Politically, socially, educationally, financially, medically, and spiritually, we were adrift in the perfect storm. Over and again, people remarked that they could "feel" the prevailing sadness, hopelessness and darkness.

We desperately needed hope.

In this context, a small movement started of people putting up their Christmas trees in *September*. Most retail stores wait until late October or early November to begin their Christmas push. But people started getting ready for Christmas much earlier. They needed Christmas. Because Christmas is "the most wonderful time of the year."

More than eight out of 10 people claim Christmas as their favorite holiday. People love decorating their home, giving gifts, watching classic movies on television, celebrating with friends and reflecting on nostalgic memories that Christmas calls to mind. For most people, Christmas is a magical mixture of beauty, curiosity, mystery and history. And we long for this.

In the worst of times, we search for a sense of wonder.

However, the wonder of Christmas isn't twinkling lights, a winter snow, homemade desserts or a decorated tree. What makes Christmas so full of wonder is that God stepped into our world and came near to us. The most wonderful time of the year celebrates the most wonderful moment in time.

## MAIN STREET BETHLEHEM

In the modest little town of Burnet, Texas, about an hour northwest of Austin, you can take a trip back in time to the birth of Jesus. Main Street Bethlehem is a magnificently produced reenactment of the ancient town and culture of Jesus' birthplace. As visitors step through the gates, they are transported back more than 2000 years. The website advertises:

*Feel the anticipation of Joseph and Mary approaching the gates, urgency quickening their steps. Pick your way through transients, peddlers, the crippled, and aged in the town's fringe. Experience the presence of animals as they affect all aspects of life in that time…camels, donkeys, sheep, goats, chickens, and doves.*

*Explore the narrow streets to faint strains of ancient music and savor the smells of fresh goat butter, campfires, and hot bread. Then immerse yourself in the din of the marketplace; the revelers in the tavern, shouted insults to and from the Roman oppressors, merchants, craftspeople, taxpayers, and beggars all seeking money, or position, or revenge.*

*Search for the inn, only to find it full (as others did long ago). Then follow the trail to the cave where a road-weary couple has moved in with the animals, their place in God's plan and secular history to be made secure on this night. For the child in their arms was the incarnation of God Himself, come to the world that all who would place their faith in Him might enjoy eternal fellowship in His presence.*

Being immersed in the sights and sounds surrounding Jesus' birth helped me appreciate an event that had become rather "ordinary." I thought about Jesus and His arrival differently… and more delightfully.

Such is the goal of this little book. *Wonder* is a daily devotional to guide you through the Advent season. Each day in December, you will be introduced to a small piece of the Christmas story designed to cultivate a greater sense of wonder. You will explore the person of Jesus, the promise of His coming, the role of His earthly parents, people who did and didn't celebrate His arrival, stars, angels and the gifts that He brings. My hope is that your heart will be overwhelmed with wonder.

## GETTING THE MOST

You will likely find this book to be a little different than others like it. It is part devotional and part doctrine, each topic no more than four pages. As a devotional book, it is intended to stir your heart. Stories and spiritual truths will help you identify with God's truth for your life. Devotionals are designed to inspire us for the day.

Doctrine, on the other hand, engages our mind. In these pages, you will be encouraged to think more deeply about the virgin birth, God's providence, spiritual warfare and the return of Christ, to name a few. Doctrine shapes our thinking so that our devotional heart is tethered to what is true. Let me encourage you not to gloss over the thinking parts to get to the feeling parts. Your wonder of Christ will grow exponentially as you consider both pieces together.

Those who take a personal tour of the Holy Land say that they will never read their Bible the same way again. A boat ride on the Sea of Galilee or an hour of silence among the olive trees in Gethsemane is enough to radically readjust what we think about the familiar stories in the Bible. At the end of the trip, travelers conclude that everything was so much more than what they had ever imagined.

Christmas is this way.

What God did in sending His Son into the world is more magnificent, more humbling, more joyful, more beautiful, more loving than anything we have previously imagined. So, each day, journey toward Christmas. Be in awe of what God did for you. And let the truth of the Savior fill your heart with wonder.

# "The world will never starve for want of wonders, but for want of wonder."

—G. K. Chesterton

# DAY 1
# THE WONDER OF THE GOSPEL

*Christmas doesn't start in the manger of Bethlehem,*
*but in the Garden of Eden.*

**C**hristmas comes every year, on the same day, like clockwork. So, why do so many people put off selecting gifts for their family and friends? A study conducted in the last year found that 79% of Americans purchase presents in the final two weeks before Christmas and 51% wait until Christmas Eve! Some people have no problem procrastinating until the last possible moment to decide what to give.

However, God didn't delay. He chose our Christmas gift thousands of years in advance.

Christmas doesn't start in the manger of Bethlehem, but in the Garden of Eden. God's glorious creation lasted two chapters until sin slithered in and ruined everything. The moment Adam and Eve took the first bite of the forbidden fruit, sin sank its teeth into the heart of humanity, turning image-reflectors into godless rebels. In Genesis 3, the universal consequences for their disobedience are announced: pain, struggle, conflict, curse and death. The beautiful communion Adam and Eve enjoyed with God was broken as they were sent away, separated by their sin.

But all was not lost. Hope was planted among the thorns of judgment. In Genesis 3:15, God announced to Satan,

"And I will put enmity
between you and the woman,
and between your offspring and hers;
he will crush your head,
and you will strike his heel."

We commonly think the first mention of the gospel in the Bible appears in *the* Gospels—Matthew, Mark, Luke and John. But God's "good news" is announced here in the first chapters of the first book of human history. Mingled among the effects of sin, God was selecting a Christmas gift for us, to be delivered centuries later. While this gospel gift was wrapped in mystery, we could know several things for certain: The gift would be a person, the gift would engage in conflict, the gift would suffer loss, and the gift would ultimately win. Thousands of years later, the angels proclaimed "good news of great joy that will be for all the people" (Luke 2:10). The gift God chose for us at the beginning was now ready to be unwrapped at the birth of Jesus.

## THE PERFECT GIFT

Sometimes people give Christmas gifts to replace something that has been broken or lost—a wristwatch with a cracked crystal, a favorite jacket left on the bus, a stereo speaker ruined in the rain. God planned the gift of the Gospel from before the beginning of the world because it's in the beginning that we discover what was broken and lost.

In the beautiful and majestic account of creation in Genesis 1-2, three things stand out. First, human beings were specially designed to reflect the image of God. While everything else in the world was "good," Adam and Eve were made "very good"—the best of the Creator's handiwork to mirror the majesty of God in the world.

Second, man and woman lived in an unhindered relationship with God. God communicated with them, gave them responsibility, and blessed them with the best of His creation. Adam and Eve lived in a perfect place and in perfect communion with God who walked in the Garden.

Third, God reigned supremely. God wasn't just creating a world but was establishing a kingdom. His command "to be fruitful and multiply" was in order to continually populate a kingdom of citizens who would rightly honor God with their lives. As King, God had the authority to give any command and to judge any command-breaker.

Three things—reflection, relationship and reign—were in the beginning. And these three things were broken or lost because of sin. When Adam and Eve chose to disobey God, their godly *re-*

## Before the first christmas was celebrated, God chose the perfect gift for the world.

*flection* was shattered, physically, ethically, emotionally, intellectually, interpersonally. Nobody is as God designed them to be. In addition, their *relationship* with God was severed. Just as Adam and Eve were cast out of the Garden, so sinners today are unable to enter the holy presence of God. And, when Satan challenged the command of God and tempted people to sin, God's *reign* was spurned. His rightful rule over our planet and its people was rejected.

So, what would God do with a reflection, a relationship and a reign that were broken? Choose a gift that would restore, redeem and recover what had been lost. Before the first Christmas was celebrated, God chose the perfect gift for people. Jesus' mission was to transform sinners so that they once again reflect the glory of God, reconcile sinners to a right relationship with God, and move redeemed people to surrender their lives under the reign of God as King. This is not just good news, but the best news ever!

## GETTING THE GIFT OF GOD

God has offered a gift—forgiveness and new life through His Son Jesus Christ. And you don't have to do anything to earn it. The Bible affirms, "For it is by grace you have been saved, through faith—and this not from yourselves, it is the gift of God—not by works, so that no one can boast" (Ephesians 2:8-9). Just as you receive a Christmas gift by opening your hands, you receive the gift of Jesus by opening your heart in faith. In other words, the person who believes Jesus is God's Son, who has paid the full penalty for their sin, will be saved.

While we can't do anything to *earn* the gift, we should do something with the gift we receive. When our spouse appreciates the gift of a sweater, they wear it. When our children appreciate the gift of a bike, they ride it. We value a gift by putting the gift to good use. If Jesus has been given to reform our reflection of God, restore our relationship to God and reestablish the reign of God over our life, then these things will become increasingly true. Jesus leads us to greater transformation into the image of Jesus, greater affection for the person of Jesus, and greater submission to the supremacy of Jesus. How is this gift of God at work in your life today?

# DAY 2
# THE WONDER OF PROMISE

*For no matter how many promises God has made, they are "Yes"
in Christ.* —2 Corinthians 1:20

Flip through this week's junk mail and you'll likely find dozens
of deals that seem too good to be true. Sure enough, when you
read the fine print you'll discover that "certain restrictions ap-
ply," "quantities are limited," "offer subject to change without
notice," or "price doesn't include shipping and handling." Each
promotion contains an asterisk—a conditional caveat.

However, you'll never find fine print in the promises of God.

Unlike fallible human beings, God is always faithful to His
Word. Therefore, every promise God makes can be trusted without suspicion. This fact should make the anticipation of a Messiah greater and the arrival of the Messiah more glorious for His
people.

We continue our journey toward Christmas with a multi-
branched family tree in Matthew 1:1-17. This is the kind of text
we might be tempted to mindlessly skip over—ancient history
with seemingly little relevance for life today. The writer announces, "A record of the genealogy of Jesus Christ the son of
David, the son of Abraham" and lists more than 40 individuals
who were "the father of" somebody else. The passage is divided
into three sections: from Abraham to David (vv. 2-6), from David

to the Babylon exile (vv. 6-11), and from Babylon to the birth of Jesus (vv. 12-16). With each name, an important truth emerges: History hinges on a promise.

Take a moment to look at just three of the names.

When Matthew mentioned Abraham, his Jewish readers would have instantly remembered God's covenant with their forefather in Genesis 12. God promised Abraham and his posterity the inheritance of a distant land, the vast multiplication of descendants and a wealth of spiritual blessings as the favored people of God. Over the next few chapters, God reaffirmed this covenant. Consider Genesis 22:16-18:

> "I swear by myself,… I will surely bless you and make your descendants as numerous as the stars in the sky and as the sand on the seashore. Your descendants will take possession of the cities of their enemies, and through your offspring all nations on earth will be blessed, because you have obeyed me."

Don't miss that the word "offspring" is singular—a significant grammatical detail. God was not simply promising that the world would be blessed through the *Jews*. God was promising that the world would be blessed through *Jesus*, the eventual offspring of the Jewish people. This is a Messianic promise.

Fast forward to the fourteenth name on Matthew's list: King David (v. 6). God had promised him "Your house and your kingdom will endure forever before me; your throne will be established forever" (2 Samuel 7:16). This wasn't only a guarantee that David's immediate family line would continue, but also that through David, God would establish an everlasting kingdom. This royal promise would be fulfilled when Jesus, descended from David's tribal line of Judah, was born "the Son of David" (Matthew 21:9) and announced the eternal Kingdom of God.

Fast forward once again to Zerubbabel, a leader of God's people after the Babylonian exile (v. 13). As the Jews sifted through the rubble to rebuild the Jerusalem temple, God spoke to Zerubbabel and promised,

> "This is what the Lord Almighty says: 'In a little while I will once more shake the heavens and the earth, the sea and the dry land. I will shake all nations, and the desired of all nations will come, and I will fill this house with glory,' says the Lord Almighty. 'The silver is mine and the gold is mine,' declares the Lord Almighty. 'The glory of this present house will be greater than the glory of the former house,' says the Lord Almighty. 'And in this place I will grant peace,' declares the Lord Almighty." (Haggai 2:6-9)

These verses are rich with Messianic hope. Whose birth shook the heavens and the earth? Who is the most desired among people everywhere? Who filled the temple in Jerusalem with great glory the moment He stepped into it? Who brought peace? The answer, of course, is Jesus.

The undercurrent of human history is that God has been making and keeping a promise to send a Savior who would graciously redeem people and gloriously reign forever.

## GOD'S PROMISES FOR YOU

What does this mean for us some 2000 years later? It means God can be trusted. We are frequently disappointed by parents, spouses, neighbors, bosses, politicians, customer service and more. But God never fails.

The Bible declares, "God is not a man, that he should lie, nor a son of man, that he should change his mind. Does he speak and then not act? Does he promise and not fulfill?" (Numbers 23:19). This means that all the promises God has made are trustworthy and true. You'll never find any fine print in His promises. So, you can trust God when He says,

- I will never leave you or forsake you (Hebrews 13:5)
- I will strengthen and help you (Isaiah 41:10)
- I will give you rest (Matthew 11:28)
- I will give you wisdom (James 1:5)
- I will forgive you of your sins (1 John 1:9)
- I will keep your salvation secure (Romans 8:37-39)

If you're not sure whether God will keep these promises, just look at Jesus. Jesus proves God's guarantee that He would never leave us, that He would help us, that He would give us rest, that He would lead us into wise truth, that He would forgive our sins, that He would keep our salvation secure, and more. Paul writes in 2 Corinthians 1:20, "For no matter how many promises God has made, they are 'Yes' in Christ."

Fortunately, God doesn't need us to be faithful in order for Him to be true. Returning to Matthew's genealogy, we are reminded that God kept His promise through Tamar's deception (v. 3), Rahab's questionable career choice (v. 5), Ruth's non-Jewish heritage (v. 5), Ahaz's corruption (v. 9), Jeconiah's disobedience (v. 11) and the apostasy of Jews that would take the nation into exile (v. 12). Paul guarantees, "If we are faithless, [God] will remain faithful, for He cannot disown Himself" (2 Timothy 2:13). Our failure or faithlessness can't prevent God's promises from coming to pass.

# DAY 3
# THE WONDER OF PROPHECY

*All this took place to fulfill what the Lord had said through the prophet.*
—Matthew 1:22

**G**reat stories take time to write. J.R.R. Tolkien used his personal experience fighting in the trenches of WWI and the backdrop of WWII to write his *Lord of the Rings* trilogy. It took him 18 years to complete the three volumes. Russian writer Leo Tolstoy took seven years to complete the 1300-page epic novel *War and Peace*. And, in 1939, *Gone with the Wind* made its theatrical debut—but only after Margaret Mitchell spent 13 years composing the four-hour classic.

The Christmas story wasn't an overnight inspiration. Long before Jesus' birth in Bethlehem, God had been writing a script, cultivating expectation in page after page of prophecy through-out Scripture. In fact, about of one-fourth of the Bible is predictive prophecy. And, while many of the prophecies had a near-term, historic fulfillment, each also pointed to a future, greater fulfillment at the coming of Christ. Prophecy is God hanging Christmas lights throughout history, shining the way to Jesus.

There are easily more than 300 prophecies identifying the coming Messiah. Consider the following selection:

- The Messiah will be born a descendent of Abraham (Genesis 22:18)

- The Messiah will be born from the tribe of Judah (Genesis 49:10)
- The Messiah will be born a descendant of David (Psalm 132:11, Jeremiah 23:5)
- The Messiah will be born of a virgin (Isaiah 7:14)
- The Messiah will be born in Bethlehem (Micah 5:2)
- The Messiah will be presented gifts at His birth from kings (Psalm 72:10)
- The Messiah will be called Immanuel (Isaiah 7:14)
- The Messiah will bless people with peace (Psalm 29:11)
- The Messiah will begin His ministry in Galilee (Isaiah 9:1)
- The Messiah will teach in parables (Psalm 78:2)
- The Messiah will be a king (Zechariah 9:9, Psalm 2:6)
- The Messiah will be called Lord (Psalm 110:1)
- The Messiah will be rejected by the Jews (Isaiah 28:16)
- The Messiah will be accused falsely (Psalm 35:11)
- The Messiah will be betrayed by a friend (Psalm 41:9)
- The Messiah will be silent before His accusers (Isaiah 53:7)
- The Messiah will be betrayed with 30 pieces of silver (Zechariah 11:12)
- The Messiah will have His hands and feet pierced (Psalm 22:16, Zechariah 12:10)
- The Messiah will be buried in a rich man's tomb (Isaiah 53:9)
- The Messiah will rise from the dead (Psalm 16:10)

Though just a small sample of prophecies, it is a remarkable list. It's conceivable that any person could fulfill one or two prophecies mentioned. But for a person to fulfill *all* of them is a statistical absurdity.

In 1958, Peter Stoner, Chairman of the Mathematics and Astronomy Department at Pasadena City College, decided to calculate the probability of one person fulfilling all the Old Testament prophecies pointing to the Messiah. The odds were so astronomical that Dr. Stoner decided to limit his calculations to just *eight* prophecies. His scientific conclusion was that for one person to fulfill just eight prophecies was $1 \times 10^{17}$. That's one person in one hundred quadrillion people!

Let's put those odds into perspective. It's estimated that 108 billion people have lived on earth since the beginning of time. Imagine all those people living on our planet *all at once*. Then imagine, not one, but *one million* of those over-populated spheres floating about in space. That's one hundred quadrillion people and only one person among all of those millions of billions of people could possibly fulfill just eight messianic prophecies. Reasonable people, like Dr. Stoner, conclude that it's a practical *impossibility*.

Yet Jesus fulfilled, not just eight, but every single one!

## HANGING CHRISTMAS LIGHTS

Some people think prophecy is only interesting to biblical scholars. But prophecy is helpful for every one of God's people in two ways: confirmation and expectation. First, prophecy gives us confirming confidence in the identity of Jesus, the Messiah. When I call a ride service to pick me up at the airport, I might let the driver know "I'm the fellow in the blue blazer and tan pants with the red suitcase" so that he locates the right customer at the curb. When Jesus was born, people could have immediately identified Him as the expected Messiah through Old Testament prophecy. Today, prophecy continues to validate the uniqueness of Jesus and gives us strong confidence that He alone is God's Son, the Savior sent to save the world.

Just as prophecy is helpful for looking backwards, it's equally helpful for looking forward into the future. For hundreds of

> The prophecies that were not yet fulfilled at Jesus' first advent cultivate great hope in God's people today as we look toward Jesus' return.

years, God revealed bits of information that assured His people that a real Messiah was coming. And prophecies not yet fulfilled at Jesus' first advent cultivate great hope in God's people today as we look toward Jesus' return. Prophecy is like a highway sign letting a tourist know that they are on the right road and that their destination is just ahead.

Some time ago, a psychology professor made the unusual discovery that spoilers don't spoil anything. While most people think that knowing the end of a story ruins the final outcome, research shows that having a little information about the final chapter actually enhances a reader's experience. Follow-up research also discovered that knowing the end helped a reader enjoy the entire story, not just the finale.

Every prophecy in the Bible is a "spoiler alert." Throughout the pages of Scripture, God announces His triumphal plan to send His Son to live, die, rise from the dead, and return in glorious splendor to defeat His enemies and reign forever. The story is still being written and we are living our own chapter of God's redemptive plan. However, we know how the story ends and unfulfilled prophecy inspires us with expectant hope.

# DAY 4
# THE WONDER OF PROVIDENCE

*At just the right time, when we were still powerless,*
*Christ died for the ungodly.* —Romans 5:6

In 1995, soon after the Iron Curtain came down in Eastern Europe, I took a group of 12 university students to Moscow, Russia. We planned a break halfway through our six-week mission to travel north to the coastal city of St. Petersburg. However, when we arrived at the train station for our scheduled departure, we discovered that we had purchased the wrong tickets and missed our train as we tried to exchange them for new ones. Our travel was postponed until the next morning when our group boarded the train for the four-hour trip. While we were in transit, I got up from my seat to stretch my legs and walk through several of the passenger cars. An English-Russian newspaper caught my eye, tossed into an empty seat. The headline announced that a bomb had exploded in the Moscow-to-St. Petersburg train the day before, killing two travelers. By missing our train, we had missed certain tragedy.

Such a fortunate event may appear to be mere coincidence. However, we know that with God, nothing is left to chance. Because of His sovereign oversight over all of creation, what may seem like coincidence is really *providence* at work.

Providence means "to see beforehand." On the back of our one-dollar bill or the Great Seal of the United States, we find the image of an eye over a pyramid. Conspiracy theorists link the symbol to Freemason secrecy, but the image is found in religious art during the Renaissance period. It represents Eye of Providence—a God who watches over all of life. God sees everything.

But providence is *more* than this. God doesn't sit passively in a heavenly recliner simply noticing all that happens on earth. He actively sustains, directs and governs every opportunity.

The word "opportunity" comes from the Latin maritime phrase "ob portu" meaning "for port." Before modern harbors, ship captains had to watch the tides before they could navigate into port. If the captain didn't seize the "ob port," the ship would have to wait for another tide, a later opportunity.

Providence is God seeing and seizing every opportunity to guide His divine purposes into port. And Christmas is a beautiful picture of providence.

According to the best evidence, Jesus was born in 4 B.C. His arrival, though a surprising miracle to his parents, was hardly unplanned in heaven. God seized a specific opportunity in time to bring His Son into the world. Notice what the Bible says:

> ...at just the right time, when we were still powerless, Christ died for the ungodly. (Romans 5:6)

> But when the time had fully come, God sent his Son, born of a woman, born under law, to redeem those under law, that we might receive the full rights of sons. (Galatians 4:4-5)

> [Jesus Christ] gave himself as a ransom for all men—the testimony given in its proper time. (1 Timothy 2:6)

Conditions on earth made the time right, full and proper for Jesus to come. Rome had secured relative peace among people,

# Prophecy is God speaking into the future; providence is God bringing His purposes to pass.

and a sophisticated road system would make global progress of the gospel possible. The Greeks had established a common language throughout the empire, making gospel communication easier. And a growing messianic hope among the Jews who longed to be free as one nation under God made gospel reception plausible. Civilization was ripe with opportunity for a Savior to come.

God was navigating the tide of events on earth to choose the most opportune time to reveal His Son to the world. Parents may give in to their children who beg to open one Christmas gift early. But God sent the gift of His Son not a moment too soon or a day too late. Prophecy is God speaking into the future; providence is God bringing His purposes to pass.

## ARRANGING THE PIECES OF YOUR LIFE

Sometimes, life can feel like God and the devil are duking it out, taking swings at one another and us with either one winning at different times. When we get into a fender bender or we throw our back out or our dog digs under the fence and runs away, it seems like the devil has the upper hand and God is getting bested by the enemy. Then the bell rings for Round #2 and God comes out swinging with an unexpected promotion, a rock-bottom clearance sale on the bike we've been eyeing or news that we're going to be a grandparent. Once again, God is winning.

But God is never not in control. Just as He arranged all the pieces so that Jesus was born at just the right time, He continues to arrange the pieces of your life today. God orchestrated your birth, ordained the day of your salvation, orders each one of your steps, and will oversee the moment of your death (Psalm 139, Ephesians 1:11, Acts 17:26). God is intimately involved in and cares about your daily life.

Sometimes, our experience of providence is *immediate*. God regularly brings beautiful sunshine and bountiful rain into each person's life (Matthew 5:45) so that even the atheist finds himself exclaiming "Thank God" without even thinking about it. "Every good and perfect gift is from above" (James 1:17), the present proof that God's providence is at work.

But, even if we don't perceive it immediately, God's providential goodness comes *ultimately*. That is, in due time, God will accomplish a good and glorious end for us and Himself. The grief of missing our train in Russia was nothing compared to the gladness we felt when we learned that we had avoided potential disaster. In every opportunity, God is at the helm steering our lives toward good (Romans 8:28).

Solomon concludes in Ecclesiastes 7:14,

When times are good, be happy;
    but when times are bad, consider:
God has made the one
    as well as the other.
Therefore, a man cannot discover
    anything about his future.

Simply put: Rejoice in prosperity and rest in adversity. We never see as clearly as God sees. His vantage point is always better. His power is always stronger. His goal is always greater. So, trust the Captain of the ship.

# DAY 5
# THE WONDER OF MARY

*I am the Lord's servant. May it be to me as you have said.*
—Luke 1:38

The worldwide COVID pandemic turned everyone and everything upside down. My son, a wedding photographer, faced multiple challenges as brides rescheduled and rearranged their ceremony plans. With gatherings limited to 10-20 people, the mandate to wear face coverings, and a restriction against serving food in public settings, wedding dreams were dashed for many young women who had been planning their perfect day since they were playing with dolls.

So, Mary's shock is understandable. The sudden appearance of an angel announcing that she would carry God's baby utterly crushed any romantic and idyllic expectations she had of her wedding day. She could have thrown up her hands in frustration, but she opened her hands in surrender instead.

Luke provides us some helpful background about Mary (Luke 1:26-38). She lived in Nazareth, a small town of about 300-400 people at the time of Jesus. She was "pledged to be married"—a commitment that was even more binding than our engagement period today. Mary was "a virgin," a young girl between 12-14 years old, and, by implication, had not yet consummated her marriage to Joseph. Though she wasn't sinless, Mary was a specially chosen instrument of God's grace. And, as a result, Mary's plans were about to change. The angel announced,

> "You will be with child and give birth to a son, and you are to give him the name Jesus. He will be great and will be called the Son of the Most High. The Lord God will give him the throne of his father David, and he will reign over the house of Jacob forever; his kingdom will never end" (Luke 1:31-33).

What a bombshell revelation! The carpet had just been pulled out from underneath the Jewish teenager and she faced the fear of breaking the news of her questionable pregnancy to her fiancé, his parents, her family, and their community. No matter how she framed her encounter with the angel, the story was likely going to end in nothing less than inconvenience, innuendo, inquisition and indictment.

But, Mary said "I am the Lord's servant. May it be to me as you have said" (Luke 1:38). The wonder of Mary is that she made herself available to God.

She reminds us of others throughout biblical history who said "Yes" to God. When God spoke to Abraham and commanded him to "Take your son, your only son, Isaac, whom you love" and sacrifice the boy as a burnt offering to God, Abraham rose early the next morning and set out in uncompromising obedience (Genesis 22). When the young boy Samuel heard God calling, he replied, "Speak, Lord, your servant is listening" (1 Samuel 3:10). And when Isaiah was caught up into the glorious presence of God, humbled and overwhelmed, he heard the voice of God enlisting a servant to go to the people. The prophet responded, "Here am I. Send me" (Isaiah 6:8). God's servants are surrendered to God's purposes.

## ANYTIME, ANYWHERE, ANYTHING

Two years out of college, I was sitting behind a computer at a state association where I worked as a graphic designer. I was days away from the deadline to send a magazine to press when God spoke to me—not audibly, but very clearly. He asked, "Is this what you'll be doing when you're old?"

At the time, it was a strange question. Since my early teenage years, I had wanted to be a graphic designer. It was my deliberate course of study in college, requiring five years to graduate because of extensive studio work. I loved my career path and was good enough to cultivate contract work on the side. This was the life I had planned for myself.

Until God called.

I was unprepared for His question. But His call was so clear that for me to avoid it would have been disobedience. I knew that, though I couldn't see the big picture just yet, I could trust God as an even better Designer who was inviting me into what He was doing. That's when I said "Yes" to pastoral ministry.

When was the last time you allowed God to disrupt your life? Perhaps your heart has been challenged with adoption, opened to a radical career change, or compelled to make a crazy financial investment in Bible translation. Maybe God is moving you to initiate a Gospel conversation or build a relationship with your immigrant neighbor. When was the last time you said "Yes" to something inconvenient, unexpected, or uncomfortable? God is calling and you need to respond with "Here am I, Lord. Anytime, anywhere, anything. Do with me as you please!"

## HOLDING ON TO HANDRAILS

Now, know this: Mary didn't *consent* without *cement*. In the middle of not knowing so much of her future, there were two things she *did* know that would strengthen her surrender. First, she knew of God's providence. When the angel said about her son, "The Lord God will give him the throne of his father David, and he will reign over the house of Jacob forever; his kingdom will never end" (vv. 32-33), Mary would have recalled God's promise hundreds of years earlier (2 Samuel 7:12-13). What God had planned, He was providentially bringing to pass. So, her "Yes" wasn't dependent on *her* being in control, but on her confidence that God was in control.

In the movie *Indiana Jones and the Temple of Doom*, there is a scene where the lead characters are lounging in the back of a plane, unaware that the pilot has dumped all the fuel and jumped out of the aircraft. When Indiana wakes, he opens the door to the cockpit and panics, "There's no one flying the plane!" Sometimes, life feels like this. But Mary knew that God is always at the controls. She banked on His providence and you can, too.

Mary also knew of God's power. How could she possibly conceive a child before marriage? How could anyone be sure the baby would be a boy? How could her son be protected from a sin nature common to all people? It all seemed so impossible! But the angel assured her, "The Holy Spirit will come upon you, and the power of the Most High will overshadow you" and "Nothing is impossible with God" (vv. 35, 37).

With God, "Where there's a will, there's a way." If God calls you to start your own business, change your college major, homeschool your kids, write a book, or lead a Bible study, He will provide all the necessary resources for you to complete His calling. Don't let the only thing standing in the way of your availability be some impossibility. God's providence and His power are the handrails you can hold onto as you follow God's path.

# DAY 6
# THE WONDER OF THE VIRGIN BIRTH

*The virgin will be with child and will give birth to a son.*
—Matthew 1:23

By all accounts, Korean-born Kim Ung-Yong was an exceptional child. He started having conversations at six months old. By the time he was one, he had learned the Korean alphabet and 1000 Chinese characters. By age four, he could read in Japanese, Korean, French, German and English. By five, he was performing complex differential equations, composed his own music, and published a best-selling book of essays in English and German. That same year, he attended a physics class at Hanyang University. He eventually earned a Ph.D. from Colorado State University when he was just 15 years old and immediately began working for NASA.

Every parent thinks their child is something to brag about. But, some children stand out among the rest. Judit Polgar was a world-class chess prodigy when she was 11. Blaise Pascal was a genius in math. Mozart was writing music by the time he was five. Yet, as exceptional as some children are, none compare to Jesus. From the moment of His angelic birth announcement, we learned that Jesus would be no ordinary child. This is because Jesus had no ordinary birth.

Matthew records the revelation of Jesus' conception, "The virgin will be with child and will give birth to a son" (Matthew

1:23). And, when Mary was told that she would bear a son, she wondered, "How will this be since I am a virgin?" (Luke 1:34). That Mary could become pregnant apart from any sexual union defies all scientific rationalism. Yet as the virgin birth survives the academic arrogance of modernism, it compels us to stand in wonder of Jesus.

## AN EXTRAORDINARY CHILD

The virgin birth is more than Jesus making a flashy entrance onto the stage of world history. How He arrived tells us about *who* and *what* He was.

First, the virgin birth confirms that Jesus was more than just a man. The landscape of religion is littered with leaders who claimed to be sent from God. Many either promoted themselves or were elevated by their followers to a divine status. They possessed charisma, knowledge or mysticism to attract others to themselves. But nothing can change the fact that they were all mere, misguided mortals.

Jesus is set apart from others in that He is God. His otherworldly origin confirms that Jesus is more than a great prophet or a good teacher. He is God who had come to earth. In fact, His whole life was bookended by the miraculous: a virginal conception and a victorious resurrection. The God who planned our salvation had personally come to perform it.

Second, the virgin birth assured that Jesus would be a suitable sacrifice. If Jesus had been born by ordinary means, He would be an ordinary man, inheriting His earthly father's sin nature. If He had been born a sinner, He would only be able to die for His own sin (Romans 6:23, Hebrews 9:22). But because Jesus was protected by the Holy Spirit (Luke 1:34), he was born a perfect human, without sin. Because His nature was holy, un-

# His whole life would be bookended by the miraculous: a virginal conception and a victorious resurrection.

blemished and pure, Jesus could become a perfect substitutionary sacrifice to die in the place of sinners.

As a perfect person, Jesus became a spotless sacrifice for other people. As infinite God, He could die for the sins of an infinite number of sinners. His extraordinary birth proved that Jesus, the God-man, was an extraordinary child.

## GOD'S MEGAPHONE

Don't dismiss the personal significance of deep-end-of-the-pool theology like the virgin birth. When Jesus was finally born, Mary "treasured up all these things and pondered them in her heart" (Luke 1:19). She looked back over the previous nine months—from the announcement to the arrival—and wondered. She mulled over the magnificence of her miraculous pregnancy.

The wonder of the virgin birth for you and me is this: God saves sinners. At the first sin, Adam and Eve attempted to cover their nakedness and hide from God. But the moment they began sewing fig leaves together, the vines started dying. They couldn't cover their own sin. For generations afterward, people observed works of the Law to get right with God. Again, the Law and human effort still fell short. No matter how hard we try, we cannot secure our salvation. One preacher lamented, "At the end of every human endeavor there is still only death."

So, God stepped in.

Jesus' supernatural birth prepares us for a supernatural rebirth. Only God could arrange the miracle of Jesus' life so that He would be born without sin. And only God can make people born again into a new life that is free from sin. John writes, "Yet to all who received him, to those who believed in his name, he gave the right to become children of God—children born not of natural descent, nor of human decision or a husband's will, but born of God" (John 1:12-13). Our first birth, decided by our parents, opens the way to this life. Our rebirth, decided by a heavenly Father and miraculously orchestrated by His Spirit, opens the way to eternal life. We're born naturally as children of wrath. We are born supernaturally as children of God. The virgin birth is God's megaphone declaring that "salvation comes from the Lord" (Psalm 3:8).

When Mary learned of God's work through her and to her, she sang a song known as "The Magnificat." Today, let her chorus be yours as you think about what magnificent thing the Lord has done for you:

> "My soul glorifies the Lord
>> and my spirit rejoices in God my Savior,
> for he has been mindful
>> of the humble state of his servant.
> From now on all generations will call me blessed,
>> for the Mighty One has done great things for me—
>> holy is his name.
> His mercy extends to those who fear him,
>> from generation to generation." (Luke 1:46-50)

# DAY 7
# THE WONDER OF JOSEPH

*When Joseph woke up, he did what the angel of the Lord had commanded him and took Mary home as his wife.* —Matthew 1:24

I t's just a few hours until the curtain is drawn on the church Christmas pageant, but Andy is sick. The 9-year-old has rehearsed for weeks with his friends to reenact the history and beauty of the Nativity. But a winter cold has sent him to bed on opening night. Andy and his parents will be disappointed, no doubt, but the show will go on. Because Andy is Joseph. And everyone knows that the story of Christmas needs Mary, the Magi, and angelic messengers. But Joseph is an extra...an expendable character.

Joseph is often relegated to the shadows in Renaissance masterpieces celebrating the birth of Christ. He has no Christmas hymns honoring his name and no mention in the Bible beyond the birth narratives in Matthew and Luke. Yet, while Joseph acted in a supporting role for the virgin and child, his life leaves an important legacy of faith.

Joseph and Mary were "pledged to be married" (Matthew 1:18), a betrothal period of one year that bound a couple together. According to custom, Joseph had been busy making marriage preparations when he learned that Mary was "found to be with child"—an unemotional, matter-of-fact record of the shocking revelation. No doubt, the news dealt a devastating blow to the young man's dreams. The future he had imagined—growing old together, raising children and grandchildren after them, celebrating milestones, basking in the Lord's blessings—devolved into shattered idealism. Sometimes, the Lord takes our lives in an unexpected direction. And it becomes desperately impossible to "straighten what He has made crooked" (Ecclesiastes 7:14).

Joseph was a righteous man (v. 19), devoted to the Jewish Law as much as his almost-bride. He could have legally and openly broken off the betrothal, leaving Mary to defend her honor among the whispering public. But he opted to divorce her discreetly. Perhaps, without creating scandal, Mary could slip into the background, a single mother raising an illegitimate child. But an angel of the Lord came to Joseph in a dream: "Joseph son of David, do not be afraid to take Mary home as your wife" (Matthew 1:20)

More than two dozen times in the Bible, God tells His people, "Don't be afraid." To the Israelites who could hear the approaching hoofbeats of the Egyptian army as they stood on the shore of the Red Sea...To His people who were about to cross the Jordan River into a promised land filled with enemies who outnumbered them...To a prophet in Babylon who was assured God would bring His people out of captivity...To a virgin in Nazareth, to Zechariah in the temple, and to shepherds in the field.

Do not be afraid.

We're urged to "fear not" because fear is our impulsive response to the unexpected, undesirable, unmanageable bends in the straightaways of life.

Joseph had a decision to make. He could allow fear to paralyze him and lead him to resort to his own strength, intuition, and resources. Or he could trust God who brings infinitely more to the table. Joseph could choose to walk away or walk by faith. Matthew writes, "When Joseph woke up, he did what the angel of the Lord had commanded him and took Mary home as his wife" (Matthew 1:24).

The wonder of Joseph was his unwavering faith.

## WHAT IS FAITH?

Faith is confidence. It's an inner certainty of what is potential (not yet) and invisible (not seen). Faith is unnecessary for me to believe that something happened five years ago or early this morning. No faith is needed for me to know that I'm typing on my laptop. It's happening right now. It's a present experience that I can see. But regarding what *may* happen tomorrow or next year, or regarding what I cannot see—this requires faith. Hebrews 11:1 is the Bible's best definition of faith: "Now faith is being sure of what we hope for and certain of what we do not see."

How does Joseph, or anyone for that matter, have faith to walk into such an unseen, unknowable future?

By looking back.

God's people have the benefit of history—how God has proved Himself faithful throughout time. Like Joseph, we can look back to the spectacular parting of the Red Sea waves or the mysterious provision of manna in the wilderness. We can remember how the walls of Jericho fell outward at a mere trumpet blast or how a boy beat a giant against all odds. We can remember fire that consumes a sacrifice on Mt. Carmel or the rescue of three courageous men in Babylon's fiery furnace. Recalling God's past work inspires faith for our present walk.

Since 2016, my wife has led a nonprofit ministry helping teen girls embrace and live out their identity in Jesus Christ. Because of COVID, THERE{4} Teen Gathering had to shift their annual in-person conference to an online, livestream experience. Then, with all the necessary pieces ready, a statewide ice storm threatened to shut down everything the week of their 2021 event. The electric power grid was unpredictable. Our church hosting the conference was managing several burst water pipes. Icy roadways and delayed flights prevented key speakers and musicians from getting into town. It was a worst-case scenario. And fear would have been a reasonable, human response.

But she remembered what God had done in previous years. Time and again, God had overcome logistical, technical, financial, and spiritual obstacles. The multitude of miracles God had performed in prior years to reach teen girls with the Gospel of Jesus could fill a book. Though "past performance is no guarantee of future results" when it comes to *earthly* investments, she could have faith that the God of her past was the God of her present. In the end, the conference was broadcast worldwide and reached more than 15,000. Faith enjoys God's reward!

In Psalm 77:11-12, the writer reflects,

I will remember the deeds of the Lord;
yes, I will remember your miracles of long ago.
I will meditate on all your works
and consider all your mighty deeds.

This is not mere nostalgia. The recollection of God's power in the past strengthens our faith for the future.

What is *your* impossible circumstance? What relationship can God not reconcile? What financial burden can He not resolve? What addiction can He not overcome? What chronic disease can He not heal? What disintegrating marriage can He not restore? Believe that what is absurd may be accomplished by the power of God. He is still able and dependable to be at work in you and *for you*. Don't be afraid. Don't walk away. Look back and then walk forward in unwavering faith.

# DAY 8
# THE WONDER OF BETHLEHEM

*So Joseph also went up from the town of Nazareth in Galilee to Judea, to Bethlehem the town of David.* —Luke 2:4

Every Christian would benefit from taking a tour of Israel and walking where Jesus walked. One of the highlights of every trip is crossing the border into Bethlehem. Today, it's a bustling city on the West Bank with its centerpiece situated on the town square: The Church of the Nativity. The 4th century basilica is co-managed by the Greek Orthodox, Catholic, and Armenian denominations and sits over the supposed site of Jesus' birth.

Bethlehem is mentioned several times in the Old Testament. It was the burial place of Jacob's wife, Rachel, and the hometown of Ruth and Naomi where they returned as widows. Like Jerusalem, the location is sometimes referred to as the City of David. But, by the time of Jesus, Bethlehem wasn't really regarded as one of the more notable cities in Israel. With no more than 300 residents, it might be too much to call Bethlehem a "city" at all. Still, God could not have chosen a better place for His Son to step into the world. The wonder of Bethlehem is that the *place* prepares us for the *person* of Jesus.

## BREAD OF LIFE

Travel to almost any country in the world and you'll find bread as the most common food staple. Pan in Mexico, naan in

India, chapati in Rwanda, baguette in France, dim sum in China. We might wish for salmon or lasagna, but if we just have some bread, that will feed our hunger. When Jesus urged people to pray, "Give us this day our daily bread," He was meaning life's necessities, not luxuries. Bread is basic to life.

In the Old Testament, as the Israelites crossed the wilderness from Egypt to Canaan, God met their need with bread from heaven. Manna (literally, "What is it?") mysteriously appeared like dew on the ground for six days of the week. God's people could gather as much as they needed, but no more. If they gathered extra, not trusting God for tomorrow's provision, what remained would be spoiled by morning. Alternatively, on the sixth day, they were commanded to gather enough for the day and an extra portion for the seventh-day Sabbath. Those who neglected to prepare for the day of rest found themselves empty-handed. This rhythm of need-provision-faith-rest continued for 40 years (see Exodus 16).

You might wonder what all of this has to do with Christmas and the little town of Bethlehem. Bethlehem is a combination of two Hebrew words: *beth* ("house") and *lehem* ("bread"). Bethlehem is literally the "house of bread." And this is significant because Jesus said, "I am the bread of life. He who comes to me will never go hungry, and he who believes in me will never be thirsty" (John 6:35). Out of the House of Bread came the Bread of Life. Jesus was born to meet our most essential need.

But, unlike God's people in the wilderness, our most important need isn't physical, but spiritual.

After Jesus multiplied the loaves and fishes for the crowd of 5000, His disciples asked Him for miracle to prove that He was, indeed, the promised Messiah. They suggested that, just as Moses called down bread from heaven to feed their forefathers, perhaps Jesus could produce a similar spectacle. Jesus responded,

"I tell you the truth, it is not Moses who has given you the bread from heaven, but it is my Father who gives you the true bread from heaven. For the bread of God is he who comes down from heaven and gives life to the world" (John 6:33-34).

Notice the shift. Moses didn't fill their empty stomachs; only God can meet human needs. The truest and best bread from heaven isn't mysterious flakes on the ground, but the Bread whom God has sent to earth—Jesus. This "Bread of Life" isn't for

> The truest and best bread from heaven isn't mysterious flakes on the ground, but the Bread whom God has sent to earth —Jesus.

the Jews only, but for the whole world. In the verses that follow, we learn that if a person trusts Jesus to meet their spiritual need, they will find Him satisfying and sufficient. And, if they have Jesus, they will have enough for sabbath rest in the presence of God forever.

Bethlehem was simply getting us ready for our deepest hunger to be met in Jesus.

## COME TO THE TABLE

Journey to the last week of Jesus' life and peer into the Upper Room in Jerusalem at a group of friends reclining at a table, celebrating the Passover meal together. Jesus took the unleavened bread, broke it and gave it to His disciples, saying, "Take this and eat it. This is my body." In that sacred moment, He memorialized His life and His death. Born in the House of Bread, the

Bread of Life would be broken to feed a starving world. The Last Supper was an invitation to feast wholly on Jesus.

Hundreds of years before Jesus was born, God spoke through the prophet Isaiah:

> Why spend money on what is not bread,
> and your labor on what does not satisfy?
> Listen, listen to me, and eat what is good,
> and your soul will delight in the richest of fare.
> (Isaiah 55:2)

What are you filling your life with today? What is feeding your starving soul? We dine at the table of media, politics, material success, business, body image, sports, technology, travel, the stock market and more. But most of the food at our feast has empty calories, insufficient for true life. Such things can make you fat but can never make you full.

Jesus is the true Manna from heaven, sent to satisfy us with the richest of fare. We discover how satisfying Jesus is by first trusting Him for our salvation. When Jesus held out the bread and said, "Take this," His followers reached out to receive what He offered. Today, Jesus offers eternal life and we "reach out" to receive Him through faith. Trust Jesus alone for eternal life and He will give you rest.

We continue to discover how satisfying Jesus is by trusting Him as our *daily* bread. The Israelites had to collect just enough bread for the day. And so, we must return to Jesus every morning, trusting Him for everything we need. He is our comfort, our joy, our hope. He gives life meaning. He is our security, our energy, our identity. He nourishes our soul. Seek Jesus again today. Find Him to be enough. Taste and see that the Lord is good…and good to *you* (Psalm 34:8).

"He who can no longer pause
to wonder and stand rapt in
awe, is as good as dead;
his eyes are closed."

—Albert Einstein

# DAY 9
# THE WONDER OF THE INN

*She wrapped him in cloths and placed him in a manger, because there was no room for them in the inn.* —Luke 2:7

A weary business traveler arrived late at a hotel only to be informed by the desk clerk that they were out of rooms. Even though he had a reservation and a confirmation number, the clerk responded, "I'm sorry, sir, but we have no vacancy."

Exhausted, the traveler replied, "If the President of the United States needed a room right here, right now, would you have one for him?"

The clerk answered tentatively, "Well, yes..."

The traveler interrupted, "Well, he's not coming, so I'll take *his* room!"

When Jesus came from heaven, the sign on our planet read "No Vacancy." Old Testament prophecy confirmed that God was sending a Messiah, but when He arrived, there was very little room for Him.

Christmas tradition imagines Mary and Joseph travelling for days from Nazareth and arriving in the dead of night at a local hotel in Bethlehem, only to be tossed out into the cold by an insensitive clerk because "there was no room for them in the inn" (Luke 2:7). Imagine being the fellow who turned away God! But this narrative detail foreshadows the difficulty Jesus would discover among those who should have been expecting Him.

We create a mental picture of "the inn"—a low budget hostel on the backstreets of Bethlehem. Some historians have offered an unexpected but interesting alternative. Luke doesn't use the Greek word for "hotel" when he mentions the inn. The word *kataluma* in Luke 2:7 is the same word used in 22:11 when Jesus asks, "Where is the guest room where I may eat the Passover with my disciples?" We know this "guest room" as the Upper Room where Jesus ate the Last Supper with His followers. Most Jewish houses were two levels—the second story "upper room" customarily used as living and sleeping space for residents and guests. The ground-level room was the kitchen and, during cold seasons, a place where owners would shelter their animals.

Now, remember that Joseph and Mary were coming to Bethlehem because the Roman census required each person to return to their ancestral hometown to be counted. When they arrived, we wouldn't expect the young couple to check in at a hotel, but to gather with family. Perhaps, however, when they showed up, many other family members were already crammed into the small upper room space. There was no room in the *kataluma* for the young man and his pregnant wife. So, they were relegated to the downstairs accommodations, or wandered outside to find a cave on the outskirts of town as tradition suggests. The point is that Jesus wasn't likely turned away by a stranger, but by the family that should have welcomed Him into the world.

John writes about Jesus, "He was in the world, and though the world was made through him, the world did not recognize him. He came to that which was his own, but his own did not receive him" (John 1:10-11). Throughout much of His life Jesus was turned away, not by outsiders, but by insiders who should have expected Him, known Him and treasured Him. Isaiah predicted this kind of reception 700 years earlier when he wrote, "He was despised and rejected by men, a man of sorrows, and familiar with suffering" (Isaiah 53:7). Sadly, Jesus confessed, "Foxes have holes and birds of the air have nests, but the Son of Man has no place to lay his head" (Luke 9:58).

Jesus still has little place to settle today.

> ## Throughout much of His life Jesus was turned away, not by outsiders, but by insiders who should have expected Him, known Him, and treasured Him.

## MAKING ROOM

A godless culture has less and less room for God (see Psalm 10:4). You'll rarely hear "in the name of Jesus" concluding a prayer at the local football game anymore. You won't find Him mentioned in retail circulars during the holiday season. His birthday isn't celebrated in public schools. Sunday is no longer a protected day of the week, having been crowded out by Little League tournaments, yardwork, and estate sales. This is hardly surprising.

More concerning is the lack of attention Jesus is getting among those in His family. To some Christians, the Savior is nothing more than a visiting houseguest rather than a permanent resident.

In a recent interview, a pastor was asked what he believed to be one of the greatest threats to vibrant spirituality today. He answered without hesitation, "Busyness." Being busy is a chronic problem among too many of God's people. Some even wear their tiresome life as a badge of honor, as if busyness is next to godliness. But our frenetic pace has left little room for Jesus. We get brief moments with Him in an occasional Sunday worship service, in a Christian song on the radio or in a prayer before a meal. But there's little margin for us to invite Him upstairs to be with us and us with Him.

The Christmas carol "Joy to the World" is still a relevant charge for us today:

*Joy to the world, the Lord is come;*
*Let earth receive her King;*
*Let every heart prepare Him room,*
*And heaven and nature sing,*
*And heaven and nature sing,*
*And heaven and heaven and nature sing!*

Make room for Jesus. This season. Today. Tomorrow. Give Him a place in your family. Give Him time in your morning. Set aside a weekly Sabbath to rest in and rejoice in Him. Read, journal, sing, be glad.

John adds, "Yet to all who received him, to those who believed in his name, he gave the right to become children of God — children born not of natural descent, nor of human decision or a husband's will, but born of God" (John 1:12-13). To those who make room, Jesus invites them to new life, eternally and experientially. He's outside, standing at the door and knocking and, "If anyone hears my voice and opens the door, I will come in and eat with him, and he with me" (Revelation 3:20). Let Him in. Give Him room.

# DAY 10
# THE WONDER OF ROYALTY

*Where is the one who has been born king of the Jews?* —Matthew 2:2

**"H**e doesn't look like a king."

The tightly bound bundle in the cattle trough struggled to break free of His wrappings. His tiny, dark eyes slowly scanned the room, taking in a new world outside the womb. A donkey brayed, startling the newborn and causing his toothless cries to pierce the midnight sky. He was so helpless. So dependent. So weak. So unspectacular to everyone other than the poor, young couple who brought Him to Bethlehem.

But, hidden among the swaddling strips was sovereignty. A visitor could not have seen it, but this baby was royalty. And His arrival into this world began His ascent to the throne.

When the wise men journeyed from the east to meet "the one born king of the Jews," they first went to Jerusalem, the capital city and the center of Israel's political and spiritual life. However, they were redirected to Bethlehem, about six miles south. This was in keeping with Micah's prophecy about the Messiah,

> But you, Bethlehem Ephrathah,
>     though you are small among the clans of Judah,
> out of you will come for me

one who will be ruler over Israel,
    whose origins are from of old,
from ancient times. (Micah 5:2)

Though Bethlehem was insignificant in comparison to other cities, it would be the birthplace of a ruler with eternal roots. That Jesus was born here set in motion the confirmation of His royal identity.

Let's take a few minutes to appreciate geography. Mary and Joseph lived in Nazareth, a town in the tribal land of Naphtali. Caesar's census decree forced them to travel to Bethlehem, located in the tribal land of Judah. When Jacob blessed each one of his sons (who became the 12 tribes of Israel), he prayed over Judah:

The scepter will not depart from Judah,
    nor the ruler's staff from between his feet,
until he comes to whom it belongs
    and the obedience of the nations is his. (Genesis 49:10)

The "scepter" and the "ruler's staff" would continually come from the tribe of Judah. And all the nations would bow before such a person. This is the language of royalty. Hundreds of years after Jacob's blessing, David was anointed king over Israel. And guess where David was born? In Bethlehem of Judah! And, through David's line, all the kings of Israel would proceed. Bethlehem wasn't just the village down the road; It was the birthplace of kings. And so, the baby in the manger possessed a royal bloodline—descended from David, of the tribe of Judah, a king for the nations.

The royalty of Jesus was confirmed over and again throughout His life. The angel Gabriel told Mary about her Son, "He will be great and will be called the Son of the Most High. The Lord

God will give him the throne of his father David, and he will reign over the house of Jacob forever; his kingdom will never end" (Luke 1:32-33). The Magi were foretold that Jesus was a king. He preached frequently about His kingdom. When Pilate asked, "Are you the king of the Jews?" Jesus agreed, "Yes, it is as you say" (Luke 23:3). He was crucified with a nameplate over His head that said as much. And, the book of Revelation announces that, when Jesus returns, He will be heralded as the "King of kings and Lord of lords" (Revelation 19:16).

Jesus isn't an authoritarian figurehead ruling only in a way that pleases Himself. He is a benevolent, perfect, righteous, and loving King who possesses absolute sovereignty as He reigns eternally. Presently, Jesus our King is seated at God's "right hand in the heavenly realms, far above all rule and authority, power and dominion, and every title that can be given, not only in the present age but also in the one to come" (Ephesians 1:20-21).

## LET EARTH RECEIVE HER KING

What is the proper disposition of citizens on earth to their heavenly King? They bow. Bending at the waist or going down to one knee makes a person physically lower than another. It's a sign of submission and surrender, humbling oneself in the presence of greatness.

For God's people today, worship is how we bow. In fact, the word "worship" in both Hebrew and Greek means "to fall down or prostrate before." Worship is not an event we attend on Sunday morning for an hour. It's whatever we do that exalts the worth of Jesus as our Lord and King. We worship with our mouths, speaking the kind of language that honors Jesus. We worship with our hands, serving others as an extension of serving our King. We worship with our giving, showing the kind of generosity that is never too much for our Lord. We worship with singing, exuberantly declaring our love and loyalty to Him. We worship with our relationships, honoring our neighbors as God's sovereign inheritance. Worship is a reorientation of all my life under the rightful rule of Jesus, my King.

The bowing of our lives in this way only occurs as the distance between our humanity and Jesus' majesty becomes greater.

## | worship is the reorientation of all my life | under the rightful rule of Jesus, my King.

John the Baptist said, "He must become greater; I must become less" (John 3:30). As the gap increases, worship ignites.

Consider Isaiah's experience, caught up in a heavenly vision of the Lord—seated on His throne, His robe trailing behind Him in the temple, a chorus of angels singing, the earth's foundations quaking, and billows of smoke curling around the sanctuary columns (Isaiah 6:1-4). John writes that Isaiah was actually encountering Jesus (John 12:41)! No Broadway production could ever match the theatrics of this awesome scene.

Overwhelmed by this reality, Isaiah cries out, "Woe to me! I am ruined! For I am a man of unclean lips, and I live among a people of unclean lips, and my eyes have seen the King, the LORD Almighty" (v. 5). As King Jesus became infinitely greater in his sight, Isaiah perceived his smallness. And the result was worship. By the time the episode was over, Isaiah had surrendered himself to God's purposes.

Look into the manger and see the kid who would be King. Jesus is our royal Sovereign, deserving of all our worship. Surrender. Fall on your knees. Let your whole life bow with all of heaven and earth to Jesus Christ who is Lord, to the glory of God the Father (Philippians 2:11).

# DAY 11
# THE WONDER OF THE STAR

*We saw his star in the east and have come to worship him.*
—Matthew 2:2

It is estimated that there are 100 billion stars in our galaxy and 100 billion galaxies in the universe. Proxima Centauri, the nearest star to earth, is 4.243 light-years or almost 25 trillion miles away. Sirius, the brightest star seen from earth, is twice the size of our sun. If you observe Sirius in the night sky, the light you see left the glowing sphere eight and a half years ago. Such majesty. So many stars. So much brilliance.

One made all the difference in the world.

The baby announcement for Jesus wasn't delivered in the mail but displayed in the heavens. Matthew writes, "After Jesus was born in Bethlehem in Judea, during the time of King Herod, Magi from the east came to Jerusalem and asked, 'Where is the one who has been born king of the Jews? We saw his star in the east and have come to worship him'" (Matthew 2:1-2). Persian astrologers noticed a cosmic phenomenon wooing them west to Jerusalem and then south to the manger. This celestial compass was God's way of inviting, not just a few foreigners, but the whole world to meet His Son.

The wonder of the Bethlehem star is that it proves God's enduring commitment to reveal Himself and His plans to the world.

Skeptics argue that God never provides sufficient proof of His existence. He leaves people grasping in the dark, having to rely on blind faith to believe. In *The Jesus I Never Knew*, even Christian author Phillip Yancey admits,

"My faith suffers from too much freedom, too many temptations to disbelieve. At times I want God to overwhelm me, to overcome my doubts with certainty, to give final proofs of his existence and his concern. I want a God without ambiguity, One to whom I can point for the sake of my doubting friends."

When I was a child, I sat in my bedroom staring at a glass of water on my desk. "God, make the glass move," I dared. It's not that I *didn't* believe, I just felt like the man who confessed to Jesus, "I do believe; help me overcome my unbelief!" (Mark 9:24). If God would just move the glass a half-inch, that would be enough to cinch my faith.

Fortunately, God *does* provide many signs—revelation to point to who He is, His Son and His work in the world. First, God reveals Himself in the SKY. Contemporary astronomers have debated whether the star at Christmas was actually a star at all. Some have speculated that it was a supernova; a comet; or the conjunction of Jupiter, Venus and Mars. Whatever it was, it was visible to all.

Psalm 19:1 tells us, "The heavens declare the glory of God; the skies proclaim the work of his hands." The fingerprints of God are all over creation. Paul writes that, from the beginning, God has been showing Himself through what has been made (Romans 1:20). The majesty of stars scattered across the sky, the breathtaking awe standing atop the Continental Divide, the thunderous power of Niagara Falls, the exquisite beauty of the

Gossamer butterfly—all of these reveal something about our God.

Second, God reveals Himself in SCRIPTURE. For the Magi, the star made them curious but the ancient Scriptures confirmed the truth, giving them specific directions (see Matthew 3:5-6). The Bible is a remarkable document—written by 40 authors, on three continents, over 1500 years, in three languages—yet consistent

## God has given people a living and lasting record of truth so that we may know Him and the way of truth.

and accurate in everything it records. God has given people a living and lasting record of truth so that we may know Him and the way of truth.

Third, God reveals Himself in His SON. The Bible is the *written* Word of God and Jesus is the *living* Word of God (John 1:1). When a disciple asked, "Show us the Father," Jesus replied, "Anyone who has seen me has seen the Father" (John 14:8-9). The writer of Hebrews explains, "in the past" God revealed Himself through prophets at many times and in various ways, but in recent times He has revealed Himself through His Son, who is God on earth (Hebrews 1:1-3). When God wanted to show Himself, He sent Jesus.

Finally, God reveals Himself through His SPIRIT. When we place our faith in Jesus, He puts His Spirit in us to reveal more and more of Himself. Jesus said, "But the Counselor, the Holy Spirit, whom the Father will send in my name, will teach you all things and will remind you of everything I have said to you" (John 14:26).

These are not the only ways that God reveals Himself. But what we can see is that He *does* wish to make Himself known generally, scripturally, personally, and spiritually. And those who see the signs and follow them in faith are sure to discover the joy of Jesus. The chorus of "We Three Kings" confirms the blessing of trusting God's signs:

*Oh, star of wonder, star of night*
*Star with royal beauty bright*
*Westward leading, still proceeding*
*Guide us to thy perfect light!*

## FOLLOW THE STAR

Most people missed the celestial announcement of Jesus, though it was in plain sight for all to see. Don't miss God revealing Himself to you today. Sometimes, asking the simple questions, "Who are You, Lord?" and "What do You want me to do?" is enough to open our eyes and ears and heart to something new. Open your Bible to a place where the pages may still be stuck together and read a fresh word. Pray about something other than the usual grocery list of requests and see how God might open your heart to something that's on His heart. Look around you and let the created order teach you about the marvelous Creator. Close your eyes and open your ears. If the Spirit of God lives in you, He will speak and show you what is true. God promises, "You will seek me and find me when you seek me with all your heart" (Jeremiah 29:13) and, when He does, you need only to follow the star.

# DAY 12
# THE WONDER OF THE MANGER

*She gave birth to her firstborn, a son. She wrapped him in cloths and placed him in a manger.* —Matthew 2:7

I am taking a break from writing this chapter to go visit my grandson who was born just hours ago. There are strict visitation rules in place at the hospital: temperature checks in the lobby, hand sanitizer at the door, face masks, a one-guest limit. Baby Otto is snugly wrapped in a clean blanket, a knit cap covering a beautiful black mop of hair. When my son or daughter-in-law needs a break, our newest family member will be gently placed in a bassinet, wheeled to a nursery where he'll get round-the-clock attention.

The sanitized, secure surroundings of my grandson's birth stand in stark contrast to the humble, hay-filled wooden box that held God's Son. Unpack your family nativity set each Christmas and a crudely carved cradle is almost certainly among the standard pieces including wise men, shepherds, cows, and sheep. The "manger" is a trough traditionally used to hold fodder for livestock. We picture Jesus' manger in a barn or a modest lean-to. It's such a sentimental symbol of Jesus' humility and His family's poverty.

Most of all, it's a reminder of His ministry.

The wonder of the manger tells us so much about Jesus' mission.

## THE TOWER OF THE FLOCK

Just outside Bethlehem, on the road connecting the little town with Jerusalem, stood the Migdal Eder, the "Tower of the Flock." This circular stone structure had been built for shepherds to get a better vantage point overlooking their flocks so they could protect their sheep from robbers and natural predators. The Migdal Eder has three, significant historic connections:

As Jacob and his wife, Rachel, approached Bethlehem, she went into difficult labor and died as she gave birth to her son, Ben-Oni, which means "Son of Sorrow." The boy's name was later changed to Benjamin, which means "son of the right hand." Jacob ended up lingering in that area for a while, pitching his tent beyond the Migdal Eder (Genesis 35:16-21).

In Micah 4:8, the prophet announced a godly king who would restore God's people and conquer evil. This messianic leader would bring peace and establish God's rule among the nations. Jewish tradition believed that the Messiah would be first announced at the Migdal Eder.

During the time of Jesus, the pastureland around the Migdal Eder was used to raise special sheep—lambs for the temple sacrifice and Passover observance. Once a lamb was born, the lamb would be kept in the Migdal Eder until religious representatives could qualify the future sacrifice as clean and unblemished. Often, the shepherd would wrap the newborn sheep in strips of cloth to protect it from scrapes or breaks that would render it unfit for an offering.

Don't read any further until you have completely grasped the gravity of these three references—the birthplace of the "Son of Sorrow," the place where the Messiah will be announced, and the place where Passover lambs are birthed. Now imagine Mary and Joseph being turned away from a cozy shelter in town and making their way to this notable landmark on the outskirts of Bethlehem. Could there be any more profound place for Jesus to be born than at the Migdal Eder? Consider the following connections to the person and purposes of Jesus.

When Jesus approached the Jordan River at the start of His ministry, John the Baptist called Him "the Lamb of God, who takes away the sin of the world!" (John 1:29). This was a meaningless, if not confusing, comment apart from the context of temple worship and sacrifice.

The Jewish Passover was an annual feast observed by the Jews to commemorate God's rescue from Egypt. The Israelites had to slaughter a lamb without defect and brush its blood over the doorposts of their home to be saved (Exodus 12). In the New Testament, the Apostle Paul refers to Christ as "our Passover lamb" (1 Corinthians 5:7). The Last Supper that Jesus ate with His disciples was a Passover meal. And, the following afternoon, Jesus died on the cross at the exact time of day when Passover

## Jesus was no ordinary man. He was the unblemished, sinless offering whose blood was shed for the sins of the world.

lambs were brought from Bethlehem and slaughtered in the Jerusalem temple.

Jesus was no ordinary man. He was the unblemished, sinless offering whose blood was shed for the sins of the world. He was the Son who had come from the Father's "right hand." But He would be "despised and rejected by men, a man of sorrows, and familiar with suffering" (Isaiah 53:3). As Messiah, His arrival was announced first at the Migdal Eder, to shepherds in the field — news of peace, victory, restoration and great joy for all the nations. And when the shepherds were told to find him swaddled and lying in the manger, they would have known exactly where to go: to the feeding trough inside the Watchtower of the Flock. Because that's where perfect sacrificial lambs were kept until it was time for them to be offered to God.

The manger prepares us for Jesus' ministry. He was born to die.

## SHEEP AND SHEPHERD

Before we leave the Migdal Eder, a final observation is worth noting. The sheep were below while the shepherds stood watch above. Jesus is not only the Lamb of God who has come to earth below, but He is also our loving shepherd in the heavens above. In this metaphorical shift, *we* are the sheep of God's pasture (Psalm 100:3) and Jesus is the Good Shepherd who continually watches over us (John 10:11, 14). As such, Jesus knows us (John 10:14-15), calls us (John 10:27), secures us (John 10:29) and provides everything for us (John 10:28). When predators come after the flock of God, He is our Defender.

So, look again into the manger, that rough-hewn makeshift crib. Tucked inside is a lamb that has been born for a purpose. He is perfect in every way—a swaddled sacrifice awaiting the Passover when His blood will be brushed over the doorframes of human hearts. He's not the one who is desperate and helpless. We are. But, in time, He will become an atoning sacrifice for sinners. And He is not only the sheep who saves but is the Good Shepherd who watches over all of those who have trusted Him in faith.

# DAY 13
# THE WONDER OF WISE MEN

*After Jesus was born in Bethlehem in Judea, during the time of King Herod, Magi from the east came to Jerusalem.* —Matthew 2:1

**N**o telling of the Christmas story would be complete without Magi crossing the desert between Babylon and Israel. Riding single file on camelback, the caravan is silhouetted against the moonlit sky as they follow a star and ancient prophecies to the birthplace of a new king. There is much mythical folklore that surrounds these royal visitors, but there are a few things about them we can know for certain.

The biblical text refers to the wise men as Magi (Matthew 2:1). The Medo-Persian word *magus* is connected to an Iranian root word meaning "powerful" or "rich." The Magi were a distinguished caste of priests or astrologers serving in the highest levels of the kingdom where they lived. Like the advisers who consulted with Pharoah during the time of Moses (Exodus 7:11, 22) or Nebuchadnezzar during the time of Daniel (Daniel 2:2), they were likely practiced in the magical arts, revered as mediums of their gods.

Matthew notes that they were "from the east," probably from the region of ancient Babylon in northern Arabia. Perhaps stories about a coming Messiah had been passed down from the Jews held in captivity in that region hundreds of years before. Depending on where they started, they could have travelled from

100 to 300 miles to reach Jesus, a journey that would have taken anywhere from three days to several weeks.

Tradition has three wise men coming to meet Jesus. In fact, they are named and described: Gaspar, from Sheba, wears a green cloak and a gold crown with jewels; Melchior, from Arabia, has a long white beard that flows down his golden robe; and Balthazar, from Egypt, has dark skin and a purple tunic. Truth is, the Bible only mentions three *gifts*—gold, frankincense and myrrh—and the rest has become legend.

While our nativity pictures the wise men standing or kneeling at the manger while animals lounge in the shadows of the stable, the visitors likely didn't arrive until one to two years after Jesus' birth. When Matthew records, "they went on their way, and the star they had seen in the east went ahead of them until it stopped over the place where the child was" (Matthew 2:9-10), he doesn't use the familiar word for "infant." Jesus is older now. Moreover, he writes that the Magi arrive at "the house," not the manger (v. 11). And, when Herod learns that these foreigners had come to meet a new king, he launches his murderous attack against the boys in Bethlehem who were two years old and younger, an unnecessary plan if Jesus had just been born just a few days earlier.

Having established a little background, what do we make of these foreigners? What place do they take in the Christmas story? The answer is found in their journey; not a geographical one, but a spiritual one. The wonder of the Magi is the road they travel to meet Jesus—a way each person is invited to take.

## THE JOURNEY TO JESUS

The journey to Jesus can be described in four steps. It begins with REVELATION. God put a star—a beacon of light in the sky—to lead faraway people to a face-to-face encounter with Jesus. Today, God reveals Himself *generally* to all people in all places through creation, human conscience and unexpected blessings to everyone, no matter what their spiritual condition. God also reveals Himself *specially* through Scripture, signs and miracles, and the words and works of Jesus. God's revelation is because God wishes to be known. If the wise men had ignored the signs, they would have missed meeting Jesus Christ. No one comes to God without God revealing Himself and the way.

The next step on the spiritual journey requires SUBMISSION. The Magi weren't nobodies. They enjoyed significant standing in their culture. Yet Matthew writes, "On coming to the house, they saw the child with his mother Mary, and they bowed down and worshiped him" (v. 11). They were great, but Jesus was greater. They humbled themselves and bowed down to Jesus as Lord and King. What a stark contrast the wise men were to Herod and the citizens of Jerusalem who were disturbed when they read the headlines of Jesus' birth (v. 3) because they feared that their quiet lives were about to be turned upside down.

All of us are kings and queens, presiding over our little kingdoms and queendoms, deciding each day who will sit on the throne of our life. No one comes to Jesus with their chest puffed out, arms folded, and nose held high: "Look how great I am! I don't really need you! I'm smart, strong and sufficient!" We must stoop in submission.

In the Church of the Nativity, in Bethlehem, a queue line inches toward a little doorway, just to the right of the Greek Orthodox altar. As they descend the narrow steps through the doorway, each visitor must bend down. And when they come to the little inset, traditionally thought to be the spot where Jesus was born, each must get on their knees to peer inside. This is the humble posture of everyone who comes to Jesus. Submission.

The third step in our spiritual journey is EXPRESSION. The Magi were not passive spectators to the Christmas miracle. They responded in very active ways. Their initial response was gladness: "When they saw the star, they were overjoyed" (v. 10). Like Mary and the angelic chorus before them, they expressed great joy in having discovered the rich treasure of Jesus! Christians are the happiest people because they have encountered Him who is the source of their greatest gladness.

Their gladness was accompanied by glory: They bowed down and worshipped Jesus (v. 11). The word "worship" means "to kiss" or "adore." Those who meet Jesus fall in love with Him and their heart affections are turned toward Him. They don't merely think Jesus is great but believe that nothing else compares to Him.

And their glory was accompanied by giving: "Then they opened their treasures and presented him with gifts of gold and of incense and of myrrh" (v. 11). These gifts were a tangible expression of their love for Jesus. God's people open their hands and surrender everything to Jesus Christ.

This brings us to the final step in the spiritual journey: TRANSFORMATION. This is not so much a "step" as a new, ongoing reality. Matthew writes about the wise men, "And having been warned in a dream not to go back to Herod, they returned to their country by another route" (v. 12). After a person encounters Jesus Christ, their life takes a different route. Their allegiances, opinions, values and priorities are reformed. It's not so much a *decision* we make as it is a complete *revision* of our life.

Where is the pin dropped on the map of your spiritual journey? Are you on the way to meet the Savior? If you have encountered Him, are your hands open in surrender? Is your heart opened with ecstatic gladness, glory and giving? Are you walking in a new way? Take the next step. Follow the wise men.

# DAY 14
# THE WONDER OF A GIFT

*Then they opened their treasures and presented him with gifts of gold and of incense and of myrrh.* —Matthew 2:11

**M**y family still talks about the Christmas when my grandmother gave my brothers and me gifts that she insisted the three of us open at the same time. Apparently, Nana had enrolled in a ceramics class and we were about to be the beneficiaries of her handiwork. I searched through the Styrofoam and tissue paper of my present to discover an angel, sitting with wings spread and lightly glazed. It was an odd gift for a teenage boy, but no doubt thoughtful and personal. My older brother also received an angel, leaving little mystery as to what was in the third box. However, when my younger brother opened his gift, he discovered a squirrel, sitting on his back feet with a bushy tail, holding an acorn. What followed was a moment of confused silence. Then the room erupted with laughter. In the years since, Nana's ceramic squirrel has been affectionately passed from house to house as an instrument of family unity.

Reading the Christmas story more than 2000 years after the event might raise eyebrows at the gifts the wise men brought with them to Bethlehem. Surely, Mary could have used a portable crib, cozy blankets or one of those baby backpacks to carry Jesus back to her hometown. But the Magi "opened their treasures and presented him with gifts of gold and of incense and of myrrh" (Matthew 2:11). Tradition notwithstanding, these three presents are unexpected. But the wonder of the gifts given to Jesus look forward to the gift of Jesus given to us.

## A PERFECT GIFT

What do you get a God who has everything? Jesus didn't *need* anything, yet each of the three gifts was perfect. Gold was the perfect gift for a king. Though not apparent to everyone, the Magi knew Jesus had been born a king and gold was the currency of royalty, filling treasuries to fund kingdom expansion. Throughout His life, Jesus promoted His imminent Kingdom and urged people to receive Him as their King (Matthew 4:17).

Frankincense was the perfect gift for a priest. In the Old Testament, temple priests would stoke the fires of incense that represented the prayers of people to God. In the same way, Jesus came as our great high priest to make Himself an offering to God on our behalf (Hebrews 4:14-16).

And myrrh was the perfect gift for a Savior. The sap-like resin was used for perfume, for cleansing, as an anesthetic, and most notably, for preparing bodies for burial. At the beginning of His life, people were already preparing Jesus for His death when He would give Himself as a Savior for the world (John 19:39).

In retrospect, the three gifts aren't very strange at all. Each anticipates Jesus' redemptive ministry as our reigning King, priestly Advocate, and sacrificial Savior. And, just as the wise men freely gave their treasure to Jesus, so Jesus came to freely give the treasure of eternal life with Him to each one of us.

There is an interesting connection between chapters three and four in John's Gospel. In chapter three, Jesus meets a man of great reputation named Nicodemus. In chapter four, He meets an unnamed woman of questionable repute. Nicodemus is a notable

Jew; the woman is a despised Samaritan. Nicodemus is religious; the woman is an outsider to the truth. Nicodemus came to Jesus at night; the woman came to Jesus at midday. Yet, with all their differences, the common theme of both chapters is the gift of God. Jesus tells Nicodemus, "For God so loved the world that he gave his one and only Son, that whoever believes in him shall not perish but have eternal life" (John 3:16). Then He says to the woman, "If you knew the gift of God and who it is that asks you for a drink, you would have asked Him and he would have given you living water" (John 4:10). God has given a soul-satisfying gift to the world.

That gift is Jesus.

## THE GIFT OF JESUS

Every grade school child remembers the dreaded fundraiser—selling candy bars, popcorn or magazines to raise money for their sports team or club. To maximize sales, the fundraising company typically offers incentives at various levels. Sell 25 candles to get the prize of a whistle. Sell 50 to get a Frisbee. A hundred sales will earn a gift of spy binoculars. And the top seller gets a pizza party for themselves and 10 friends. The gifts are not gifts at all because they are earned. They are simply rewards for good performance.

The gift of God, however, is one hundred percent free. Jesus offers salvation to sinners who can do nothing to earn God's favor. This gift is available to everyone with no strings attached. Paul celebrates, "For it is by grace you have been saved, through faith—and this not from yourselves, it is the gift of God—not by works, so that no one can boast" (Ephesians 2:8-9). Jesus wants to reign over you as your King, make you a pleasant fragrance before God as your Priest, and give Himself as an atoning sacrifice for sin as your Savior. And you don't owe Him anything. Salvation is all grace.

When we receive the gift of Jesus, we also receive coordinate benefits from being "in Christ." We receive the gift of righteousness (Romans 5:17), a right standing before God based on what Jesus Christ has done for us. We receive the gift of the Holy Spirit (Acts 1:4) who lives inside of each Christian and guides them into new life with God. And we receive individual spiritual gifts (1 Corinthians 12:1-11) that enable us to serve God with our lives. No wonder God's people ought to be like a child who wakes up on Christmas morning to discover a new bike beside the Christmas tree! We exclaim, "Thanks be to God for his indescribable gift!" (2 Corinthians 9:15).

There is a story about the riches of Jesus from a source that has since been forgotten. Long ago, there ruled in Persia a wise and good king who loved his people. He wanted to know how they lived and the hardships they endured. So, on occasion, he would dress in the clothes of a working man or a beggar and visit the homes of the poor. No one imagined that he was their ruler. One time he visited a very poor man who lived in a cellar. The disguised king ate the coarse food the poor man ate and, while together, spoke cheerful, kind words. Sometime later he visited the poor man again and disclosed his identity, saying, "I am your king!" The king expected the man would surely ask for some gift or favor. Instead, he said, "You left your palace and your glory to visit me in this dark, dreary place. You ate the morsels of food I ate, and you brought gladness to my heart! To others you have given your rich gifts. To me you have given yourself!"

The wise men thought they were bringing gifts to Jesus. They were unaware that Jesus was God bringing a gift to them. And us. Jesus brought us what we all needed—eternal life with God. He is our free gift with so many benefits that we shout for joy because of Him. God didn't send us stuff. He sent His Son! The richest gift of Christmas is that our God has given Himself.

# DAY 15
# THE WONDER OF ANGELS

*Are not all angels ministering spirits sent to serve those who will inherit salvation?* —Hebrews 1:14

**V**ividly etched in my memory are the animated specials on television that marked the official nearness of Christmastime. And it wasn't just the stories but the storytellers that were so unforgettable. I can still hear Burl Ives narrating the story of *Rudolph the Red-Nosed Reindeer*, Fred Astaire telling viewers that *Santa Claus Is Coming to Town*, and Jimmy Durante singing us through *Frosty the Snowman*. More recently, Bob Newhart as Papa Elf helped us travel with *Elf* to find his father in New York City.

Read the Christmas story in Matthew's and Luke's Gospels and you'll hear an unmistakable narrative voice, not from the writers alone, but from another, higher up. Angels are the reoccurring thread moving us from announcement to birth and beyond. The angel Gabriel appeared to Zechariah, announcing the unexpected birth of John the Baptist who would become the forerunner to Jesus (Luke 1:11). Next, the angel told Mary that she would miraculously conceive the Son of God (Luke 1:26). Joseph was alerted by an angel to God's plan and was encouraged to courageously keep his wedding commitment to Mary (Matthew 1:20). An angel, joined by a larger angelic host, announced Jesus' birth to shepherds in the field (Luke 2:9, 13). An angel warned Joseph to escape to Egypt to protect the baby Jesus from Herod

(Matthew 2:13) and an angel alerted him as to when the coast was clear to return (Matthew 2:19). Angels were God's messengers sent to help people fully grasp what God was doing.

The wonder of angels is their service to God's people so that we might receive the blessing that God has given us.

## ANGELOLOGY 101

Contrary to popular belief, people don't become angels when they die. Angels are spiritual brings, created by God in the beginning. When Satan sinned, he dragged a third of the angelic realm into His rebellion (Revelation 12:4) and these fallen angels became known as demons. The remaining angels have various positions and functions in the heavenly realms. Archangels—Michael and Gabriel—engage in spiritual combat and deliver messages on behalf of God. Cherubim guard the holiness of God (Exodus 25:18) and seraphim (literally, "burning ones") are worshipping angels who continuously praise God. Often, when angels appeared, people became terrified because the sudden appearance of these spiritual representatives was associated with divine judgment. But, in the Christmas story, angels bring good news of great joy for everyone.

Hebrews 1:14 tells of the special relationship between angels and people: "Are not all angels ministering spirits sent to serve those who will inherit salvation?" Imagine, God has commissioned His heavenly hosts to assist those who are marked for eternal life. The Bible isn't clear regarding guardian angels, but all angels come to the aid of God's people.

What makes the ministry of angels much more amazing is that they declare a salvation they have always *expected* but can never personally *enjoy*. Angels have watched throughout history, earnestly seeking the time when the promised Messiah would

# we can receive a gift that angels cannot fully grasp.

come to earth (1 Peter 1:10-12). And, when Jesus was born, the heavens broke open in symphony, "Glory to God in the highest, and on earth peace to men on whom his favor rests" (Luke 2:14). But, while they sang what was true, the salvation coming was something angels could only observe from a distance. You see, good angels don't *need* to be saved and bad demons can *never* be saved. Jesus came to make bad people better—to help sinners who are at war with God experience eternal peace. We can receive a gift that angels cannot fully grasp.

## HOW GREAT OUR JOY!

If angels rejoice at what they cannot fully realize, how much greater ought to be the joy of those who personally encounter the blessing of Jesus Christ? The German carol "How Great Our Joy" reminds us,

> *While by the sheep we watched at night,*
> *Glad tidings brought an angel bright.*
> *How great our joy! Great our joy!*
> *Joy, joy, joy! Joy, joy, joy!*
> *Praise we the Lord in heav'n on high!*
> *Praise we the Lord in heav'n on high!*

An exuberant, explosive joy should become our daily chorus because of the gift of Jesus and the beautiful peace that He brings to our enemy heart. Our Redeemer descended from heaven, defeated our enemy, died to pay our penalty and declared us children of God, heirs to an eternal Kingdom! That's something to sing about!

It might help to know that the angels' joy erupted from *speaking* the news, not just seeing it happen. In other words, their joy was completed as they announced to others that Jesus Christ was born. In the same way, your joy becomes full as you "Go Tell It on the Mountain." Sharing who Jesus is and what He has done for us multiplies our gladness. In his *Reflections on the Psalms*, C.S. Lewis explains this connection between joy possessed and joy expressed:

> I think we delight to praise what we enjoy because the praise not merely expresses but completes the enjoyment; it is its appointed consummation. If it were possible for a created soul fully to 'appreciate,' that is, to love and delight in, the worthiest object of all, and simultaneously at every moment to give this delight perfect expression, then that soul would be in supreme blessedness. To praise God fully we must suppose ourselves to be in perfect love with God, drowned in, dissolved by that delight which, far from remaining pent up within ourselves as incommunicable bliss, flows out from us incessantly again in effortless and perfect expression. Our joy is no more separable from the praise in which it liberates and utters itself than the brightness a mirror receives is separable from the brightness it sheds.

Don't miss the opportunity to increase your joy. If the angels can sing about what they can never possess, the praise of those who have personally encountered Jesus must be louder. And, when you "declare the praises of Him who brought you out of darkness into His wonderful light" (1 Peter 2:9), you will, in fact, become a bit more like the angels, narrating the story of Jesus and serving those destined to meet Him.

# DAY 16
# THE WONDER OF ANTICIPATION

*Even angels long to look into these things.* —1 Peter 1:12

S ome time ago, Timex (the watch company) published the results of a survey intended to find out where our time goes.
They discovered that, on average, people wait seven minutes for
a cup of a coffee, 32 minutes at the doctor's office, 20 minutes a
day in traffic, and 13 hours each year on hold for customer service. So much waiting for so little benefit. Perhaps this is why
patience is so hard to come by. Because the payoff is seldom
worth the wait.

The advent of Christ was the most anticipated event in history. The Bible records how many waited with hopeful expectancy:

> Concerning this salvation, the prophets, who spoke of the
> grace that was to come to you, searched intently and with the
> greatest care, trying to find out the time and circumstances to
> which the Spirit of Christ in them was pointing when he pre-
> dicted the sufferings of Christ and the glories that would fol-
> low. It was revealed to them that they were not serving
> themselves but you, when they spoke of the things that have
> now been told you by those who have preached the gospel to
> you by the Holy Spirit sent from heaven. Even angels long to
> look into these things. (1 Peter 1:10-12)

Moments after sin wrecked all that had been created, God promised a rescue operation (Genesis 3:15). This salvation plan began to take shape in each period of history. The preservation of a family through a great flood anticipated a remnant inheriting a renewed earth. The covenant made with Abraham anticipated a kingdom of set apart people, specially loved by God. The exodus under Moses anticipated a liberation from enemy bondage. The Temple laws and sacrifice anticipated God's standard that could be atoned for by substitution. David's rise to the throne anticipated a shepherd-king who would rule in righteousness and goodness. The prophets anticipated a spokesperson from God who would show the way back to God. Each epoch hinted at the Messiah.

And, as the anticipation built, those in heaven and on earth tried to make sense of the times. Prophets who knew all of the scriptural clues regarding the Messiah sought to connect the dots to determine if His advent was near. And angels, who had been bystanders to the Fall, the promises, and the rise and decline of God's people, searched as history unfolded to see if the time was near for Jesus to step onto the world stage.

For children, the wonder of Christmas has always been "What?" "What's in the present? What did you get me?" I spent countless hours under our Christmas tree, shaking, weighing, analyzing each package to figure out *what* was inside. I knew *when* we would open our gifts—Christmas morning, December 25. That was a guarantee. But the *what* was always a mystery.

For those in heaven and on earth watching God at work through history, the question was never *what*, but *when*. The gift was the Messiah. But they had to wait with eager anticipation to learn exactly when He would come. And, when Jesus was finally born, they could finally rejoice, "This is what we've been waiting for!"

> For those in heaven and on earth watching God at work through history, the question was never *what*, but *when*.

## STILL SEARCHING

We all have the benefit of living on this side of Christmas. We look back and see that Jesus arrived at just the right time, we see the fullness of His life and we see His finished work on the cross. And as those impacted by Jesus' first coming, we join all of heaven looking forward to His return. More than a few times, the Bible highlights this future hope. Two passages are particularly important.

In John 14:2-3, Jesus encouraged His disciples with a promise,

In my Father's house are many rooms; if it were not so, I would have told you. I am going there to prepare a place for you. And if I go and prepare a place for you, I will come back and take you to be with me that you also may be where I am.

The language Jesus used was familiar to Jewish betrothal customs. A young man would go to his beloved's home to request her hand in marriage. Now engaged, he would say to his bride-to-be, "I am going to prepare a place for us and then I will come to get you." He would return to his family homestead to begin building a honeymoon home for the both of them. When *his father* agreed that the house was ready, he would send his son to get his bride.

Jesus has gone to "His Father's house" and is preparing a special place for His bride—the people of God. When God the

Father decides (Mark 13:32), Jesus will return to sweep the church off her feet and bring every believer home. This is not a possibility but a promise!

A second, related passage is found in Matthew 25:1-13. The Parable of the Ten Virgins tells the tale of a bridegroom coming to get his bride and arriving at her house to a mixed reception. Five of the bridesmaids were ready with their oil lamps full and wicks trimmed to join the celebratory procession. Five others were caught off guard. Unprepared for the groom's surprise arrival, they rushed off to get more oil and missed the entire wedding.

The lesson, of course, applies to us today. Be ready for Jesus' return. Live with daily expectancy of His coming. His second advent will be like the first. We know that He's coming back but we don't know exactly when. Live like the prophets and angels, intently searching and ever-longing. The chorus of worship leader Chris Tomlin's "Even So Come" is a perfect anthem for those living with such anticipation:

*Like a bride*
*Waiting for her groom*
*We'll be a church*
*Ready for You*
*Every heart longing for our King*
*We sing*
*Even so come*
*Lord Jesus come.*

# DAY 17
# THE WONDER OF SHEPHERDS

*They spread the word concerning what had been told them about this child.* —Luke 2:17

On January 18, 2020, a letter was posted to @sussexroyal, the official Instagram account of the Duke and Duchess of Sussex. It was a statement from Her Majesty the Queen announcing the departure of Harry and Megan as senior members of the royal family and their upcoming plans to move to the United States. Not surprisingly, the post went viral, gaining more than 1.7 million responses.

Some news is too important *not* to share.

And, if the announcement of a prince and princess leaving their home is noteworthy, how much more significant is the report of a King who has left His home in heaven to come to earth? The wonder of simple shepherds in the field is that they received, rejoiced in and reported the good news of Jesus' birth.

The night air was brisk for the band of shepherds huddled together in the pastureland outside of Bethlehem. Resting by the campfire, an occasional bleating of sheep breaking the silence, they shared stories and gossip from the day or recounted ancient tales of national history. They guarded no ordinary flocks. These were lambs raised for the Temple sacrifice—premium livestock requiring round-the-clock protection from animal and human predators. Some may have stood watch from a higher vantage point in the Migdal Eder. The rest took turns at one of four watches throughout the night. Jewish tradition held that when the Messiah arrived, he would come at midnight.

Suddenly, "An angel of the Lord appeared to them, and the glory of the Lord shone around them, and they were terrified" (Luke 2:9). The beauty of the star-flung sky became exponentially more brilliant as an angelic messenger descended from above. The otherworldly phenomenon made the men shrink back in heart-pounding terror. Never had they been more aware of their humanity and vulnerability.

But the angel put them at ease: "Do not be afraid. I bring you good news of great joy that will be for all the people. Today in the town of David a Savior has been born to you; he is Christ the Lord" (vv. 10-11). The Greek word *Christos* ("Christ") is also the Hebrew word *Mashiach* ("Messiah"). The very first people to learn of the Messiah's arrival were peasant countrymen in the fields looking after Passover lambs. When they learned the good news, they left their flocks to search Bethlehem for the Savior. They must have been so convinced that the Savior of Israel had come that they willingly abandoned their posts, convinced that temple sacrifices were no longer needed because the true Lamb of God was born.

This was world news worth posting.

## SOMETHING TO TALK ABOUT

Having received the news of Jesus' birth, the shepherds rejoiced. They glorified and praised God for everything they saw and heard (v. 20). But their praise wasn't private. Matthew writes, "they spread the word concerning what had been told them about this child, and all who heard it were amazed at what

# Their personal encounter with Jesus compelled @bethlehemshepherds to post "Just met the Messiah. Everything is about to change!"

the shepherds said to them" (vv. 17-18). Their personal encounter with Jesus compelled @bethlehemshepherds to post "Just met the Messiah. Everything is about to change!"

Very often, when people discovered Jesus, they went throughout their local community telling everyone about it. When Peter and John were arrested and commanded not to preach about Jesus anymore, they refused because "we cannot help speaking about what we have seen and heard" (Acts 4:20). In the opening verses of his first letter, John connects personal encounter with public expression,

> That which was from the beginning, which we have heard, which we have seen with our eyes, which we have looked at and our hands have touched—this we proclaim concerning the Word of life. The life appeared; we have seen it and testify to it, and we proclaim to you the eternal life, which was with the Father and has appeared to us. We proclaim to you what we have seen and heard, so that you also may have fellowship with us. And our fellowship is with the Father and with his Son, Jesus Christ. We write this to make our joy complete. (1 John 1:1-4)

If you have met Jesus, you have something to talk about. What you have seen with your eyes, heard with your ears, embraced with your heart, enjoyed with your life—this Gospel must be announced from the rooftops! Just as the shepherds were passing on news they received from the angel, so you and I are simply conduits of the good news we heard from somebody else. Let your wonder of Jesus overflow into the world.

Take a few cues from the angel's announcement to spur on your own sharing. Never forget that Jesus is "good news." Turn on the television and it doesn't take long to realize that everyone could use a little good news. People are yearning for Jesus. They just don't know it. Share the Gospel and you will bring joy to your world.

Also notice that this good news was "for all the people." Don't try to figure out who needs Jesus and who doesn't. He's for everyone—white collar and blue collar, conservatives and liberals, nationals and immigrants, wealthy and poor, educated and ignorant, successful and failures, enemies and friends. Everyone needs Jesus.

Remember, you're not inviting people into religion, but into a relationship with the living God. Jesus offers far more than rigid rule-following. He promises peace and joy through the forgiveness of sins.

Finally, let your changed life speak for itself. It's important for Christians to open their lips. But your Jesus-centered life will often preach even louder than words. Saint Francis of Assisi said, "Preach Christ at all times and if necessary, use words."

Go to Bethlehem and find your Savior. If you already know Him, return home, and tell everyone you meet what He has done for you. Post away. Make your message go viral. Perhaps someone will listen to your glorious story, be amazed, and meet the Messiah too.

Many, Lord my God, are the wonders you have done, the things you planned for us. None can compare with you; were I to speak and tell of your deeds, they would be too many to declare.

—Psalm 40:5

# DAY 18
# THE WONDER OF JOY

*I bring you good news of great joy that will be for all the people.*
—Luke 2:10

Jesus brings joy. Joy was the most frequent response to the birth of the Savior among those who first encountered Him. Elizabeth's baby leaped for joy at the presence of Mary's unborn miracle-child (Luke 1:44). Angels proclaimed "good news of great joy" to shepherds on Christmas morning (Luke 2:10). And when the wise men saw the star leading them to the king, they were beside-themselves-overjoyed (Matthew 2:10). So, it's not surprising that our favorite Christmas carols proclaim "Joy to the World," "How Great Our Joy," and "Tidings of Comfort and Joy."

If only it were that easy.

More often, the Christmas season invites anything *but* joy. Black Friday, Cyber Monday, last-minute shopping and shipping, parties on top of parties, crowds and chaos. Dr. Seuss introduced readers to a cave-dwelling misfit who loathed the people of Whoville with all their Christmas anticipation, preparation and celebration. Though *How the Grinch Stole Christmas* was written in 1957, Dr. Seuss knew the human condition too well—a condition still common among many people today. Some hearts have shrunk "two sizes too small"—desperately vacant of joy.

According to God's Word, several things can steal a person's joy. At the top of the list is suffering. Trials come to all people: loss of a job, death of a family member, chronic medical challenges, unexpected and burdensome expenses. The reason we must be reminded to "consider it all joy" (James 1:2) is because joy is the first casualty when we suffer.

Conflict with other people also robs us of joy. Paul told His fellow Christians that his joy would be full if they practiced "being like-minded, having the same love, being one in spirit and purpose" (Philippians 2:2). Alternatively, hurt, anger, division, and bitterness among relationships pulls the dark cloud of discontent over an otherwise joyful heart.

Busyness can also keep joy at bay. During the Christmas season, "there'll be parties for hosting, marshmallows for toasting and caroling out in the snow," which sounds idyllic until you have to plan the party, purchase the marshmallows, and coordinate all of the music and winter mittens for 25 kids who will go caroling in your neighborhood. The frenetic pace some people keep—not just at Christmas, but throughout the rest of the year—makes joy hard to come by.

Joy is also forfeited in religion. Rule-keeping, legalistic piety is exhausting and saps the satisfaction from our souls. When Paul wrote to young Christians who had reverted to conformity to the Jewish Law, he asked "What has happened to all your joy?' (Galatians 4:15). Similarly, when Jesus told the story of a prodigal son who had come to his senses and returned home, the older brother found no joy because he was too caught up in his own moralistic legalism.

Finally, sin sabotages our joy. Jesus said, "If you obey my commands, you will remain in my love, just as I have obeyed my Father's commands and remain in his love. I have told you this so that my joy may be in you and that your joy may be complete" (John 15:10-11). He knew that obedience to God results in freedom and joyful gladness, but disobedience brings bondage and frustration.

Suffering, conflict, busyness, legalism, and sin are joy-killers common to all people. The good news is that Jesus came to restore our joy. This the angels announced.

## GREAT JOY FOR ALL!

Jesus and joy go hand-in-hand. Paul follows his command for us to "Rejoice in the Lord always" with "The Lord is near" (Philippians 4:5-6). The nearness of Jesus produces a fullness of joy. Jesus reorients our lives away from all the things that drain our joy to Himself, who brings us overflowing joy.

For example, Jesus gives us strength to persevere in our suffering and points us toward a future hope with Him that is free from all the weariness of this world. Jesus reconciles the conflict we have with God and makes it possible for us to be reconciled to one another. Jesus offers us purpose and meaning in life so that we can slow down our feverish pace and be content with who He has made us to be. Jesus frees us from legalistic obligation and invites us into a moment-by-moment grace relationship with Himself. And, through His resurrection from the dead, Jesus provides victory over sin so that we no longer have to live in bondage to our vices. Peter expresses it so beautifully,

> Though you have not seen him, you love him; and even though you do not see him now, you believe in him and are filled with an inexpressible and glorious joy, for you are receiving the goal of your faith, the salvation of your souls. (1 Peter 1:8-9)

# "Joy is the flag flown over the castle of the heart when the King is in residence there."

When a person meets Jesus—even though it's not face-to-face—their joy-cup spills over as all of the benefits of living by faith in Him begin to work through their life. One writer expressed it this way: "Joy is the flag flown over the castle of the heart when the King is in residence there." We don't find our joy in Christmas; we find our joy in what Christmas celebrates, Jesus.

My wedding in 1989 was one of the most wonderful days of my life. On that glorious occasion, I was finally united with the girl of my dreams. Each anniversary since, I have not found my gladness in our wedding, but in what the wedding made possible: our growing and great love for one another. Similarly, the wise men didn't rejoice in the star and the angels didn't rejoice in a manger birth. Both rejoiced at what those things represented. Jesus was here.

This Christmas don't expect to find your joy in the music, movie classics, family get togethers, decorations, new recipes, or old traditions. Your joy isn't even found in these pages. There is a deeper delight to be found in Jesus. Invite Him to increase the capacity of your heart. Invite Him to reside as King over every decision, give Him every concern, trust Him with every problem, believe Him for every truth. Raise the flag of your Christmas joy!

# DAY 19
# THE WONDER OF OUR WONDERFUL COUNSELOR

*And he will be called Wonderful Counselor* —Isaiah 9:6

In the summer of 1990, I discovered why Colorado residents share a general dislike for visitors from Texas. Tiffany and I borrowed a camp Jeep to travel the backcountry trail between Lake City and Ouray. The one-way Engineer Pass is beautiful but becomes very narrow in several places. As we exited the highway and began our drive into the mountains, we passed several warnings signs, each one growing more serious. The first one read "Unpaved Road. Proceed With Caution." The next one warned "Uneven Terrain. Four-Wheel Drive Required." Several signs later, a skull and crossbones icon topped a sign alerting "Danger of Death: Absolutely No Vehicles Without Four-Wheel Drive Permitted Past This Point!" The parks department had *my* attention but had failed to get the attention of the vacationers in front of us. As we rounded one of the hairpin switchbacks, we came upon a camper stuck mid-turn. It was no ordinary vehicle, but a full-size, 35-foot RV with Texas license plates. While the husband was in the road picking up the bumper he had ripped off his vehicle trying to back up, his wife sat crying hysterically in the front seat.

They were out of their league. The couple had everything they needed to travel cross country. But they had apparently failed to pack a most essential skill for travelling through life: wisdom.

Wisdom is more than common sense or book smarts. It's more than information; wisdom is *insight*. It's the spiritual capacity to understand life from God's perspective and thereby make decisions that are true, good, and glorifying to Him. The wise person doesn't just ask, "Can I do this?" but *"Should* I do this?" Their wisdom gives them eyes to see beyond the facts to the potential life-impacting outcome of their choices.

Wisdom is "more precious than rubies, and nothing you desire can compare with her" (Proverbs 8:11). In fact, it's so priceless that, when God offered to grant any wish of the king, Solomon asked for wisdom (1 Kings 3). For this reason, the Bible urges people to "Get wisdom!" (Proverbs 4:5).

## WISDOM IS BORN

This brief introduction to wisdom is important for understanding something of Jesus' identity. Seven hundred years before Jesus was born, the southern Kingdom of Judah could hear approaching hoofbeats from the east. The Babylonians were about to seize Jerusalem, and God's people would soon find themselves in exile. However, the prophet Isaiah delivered a word of hope: A child would be born and a son would be given who would govern with justice and righteousness. And "he will be called Wonderful Counselor, Mighty God, Everlasting Father, Prince of Peace" (Isaiah 9:6-7). These titles, made famous in the majestic oratorio of Handel's "Hallelujah Chorus," point to none other than Jesus. Each will be considered in subsequent chapters, but Jesus is first called a "Wonderful Counselor."

The word "wonderful" means "full of wonder," that which is miraculous, marvelous or exceptional. When the Bible speaks of something wonderful, it almost always refers to God's work in history. Moses asked, "Who among the gods is like you, O Lord? Who is like you—majestic in holiness, awesome in glory, working wonders?" (Exodus 15:11).

A counselor is an advisor or guide—someone who has greater understanding to bring others along. So, to say that Jesus is our "Wonderful Counselor" means that He is the embodiment of divine truth who has broken into history. Jesus is God's wisdom born to us.

Indeed, when Jesus taught, people were amazed at His insight and authority (Matthew 7:28-19). Even as a young boy, Jesus conversed with Israel's Law experts, impressing them with His answers. Jesus was wise beyond His years, so it seemed. And Paul wrote that "in [Christ] are hidden all the treasures of wisdom and knowledge" (Colossians 2:3).

But this means more than just Jesus was the smartest guy in the room. As our Wonderful Counselor, Jesus shows us the truest way to the good life with God. If we want to know the best

## | Jesus shows us the truest way to the good life with God.

way for life to work, we don't search the internet, download podcasts, or listen to talk radio. You probably won't find all the best answers scrolling through your friend's social media feed. But, in Jesus, we find "the way, the truth and the life" (John 14:6). He alone holds the key to the secret vault of rich wisdom. When we follow Him, we discover the life which is truly life.

## FOOLISH WISDOM

The thing about divine wisdom is that it is often counterintuitive to what we expect in the world. Jesus' way can appear to be foolishness to those who are unacquainted with wisdom from above. For example, Jesus calls His followers to:

- Forgive and bless their enemies.
- Not assert their rights but be humble.
- Be the best by being last.
- Radically give away their resources.
- Invest in the coming Kingdom, not this one.
- Meet the needs of strangers, not just friends.

Your world will not think these principles are smart. But Jesus will tell you that they are wise and best. They are God's way, revealed to us by our Wonderful Counselor, God's Son. As you head out on the mountainous trails of life, you will need His wisdom to navigate the sharp turns ahead. Ask Jesus to give you His perspective on the decisions you must make today. Ask, seek, knock. He won't withhold His counsel from those who seek it (James 1:5). The world doesn't understand this kind of thinking. Only Jesus, who has come from heaven, can supply wisdom you need.

# DAY 20
# THE WONDER OF OUR MIGHTY GOD

*And he will be called...Mighty God.* —Isaiah 9:6

Search the topic "most powerful" and Google will populate quite an impressive list of results. The most powerful machine is NASA's Saturn V Rocket used in the Apollo program. The most powerful weapon is the Tsar Bomba 50 megaton hydrogen bomb, equal to 50 million tons of dynamite. The most powerful animal is *Balaenoptera musculus,* the Blue Whale, growing up to 400,000 pounds and more than 100 feet long. The most powerful material is graphene. A paper-thin sheet is 200 times stronger than steel and can support 14 million pounds per square inch.

No one would doubt the awesome might of such machines, materials or mammals. But the last thing a young girl would think as she looked at her baby laying wrapped in a bed of hay is "powerful." No one in Bethlehem would have thought as much. And yet, Jesus' tiny, tight, infant fists held all the power of the universe. For this reason, Isaiah would write about the coming Messiah as "Mighty God."

The Hebrew word for "mighty" can be translated as "champion" or "hero" or "warrior." The word is used dozens of times in the Old Testament to describe winners—the 30,000 warriors chosen by Joshua (Joshua 8:3), Goliath the giant from Gath

# Jesus' tiny, tight, infant fists held all the power of the universe.

(1 Samuel 17:15), or David's band of mighty men (2 Samuel 23:8). However, Isaiah wasn't looking forward to another mighty *man*, but a champion who would be born a mighty *God*.

Of course, Isaiah is speaking of Jesus.

Jesus proved His mighty power over and over again throughout the Gospel accounts. He turned water into wine, healed diseases, gave sight to the blind, restored the lame, fed the multitudes, walked on water, calmed the sea and raised the dead, just to name a few examples. The question we should ask is, "Why?" Why did Jesus perform miracles?

There is a story told of an American bodybuilder who was visiting Africa. A tribal chief looked at the visitor's impressive physique, muscles chiseled on every inch of his body. As the bodybuilder flexed his calf muscles, triceps, biceps and thighs as a display of all his hard work, the chief asked, "What else do you use them for?"

The visitor replied, "That's it. My muscles are for show."

The chief responded, "What a waste."

Indeed, if Jesus merely flexed His muscles for show, His miracles would be welcomed, but a waste. However, there are two higher reasons why Jesus' put His power on display. First, Jesus was mighty *for God*. Every wonderful work was a manifestation of the power of God that proved Jesus to be the Son of God and magnified the glory of God through the Son's ministry. In other words, Jesus' miracles were designed to make much of God. The prophet Jeremiah said about God, "You performed miraculous signs and wonders in Egypt and have continued them to this day, both in Israel and among all mankind, and have gained the renown that is still yours" (Jeremiah 32:20). Jesus exercised His mighty power for the sake of God's fame.

Jesus was also mighty for *us*. The Son of God wasn't unaware of the human need all around Him, at every place finding people sick, hungry, lost, and dead. Jesus proved that God not only knows about our challenges, but enters into our challenges to heal, feed, find, and restore. The greatest exercise of Jesus' power is His resurrection from the dead. Jesus overcame the stronghold of the grave and the power of our enemy, Satan, to offer people the hope of new life forever. This "incomparably great power" (Ephesians 1:19) that raised Jesus from the dead is offered to His people so that each of us can continually conquer the devil and win the spiritual war. Jesus is a champion who makes us victorious over sin and death. His great power is for our good.

## NOTHING IS IMPOSSIBLE FOR GOD

Children sing the ditty: "My God is so big, so strong, and so mighty, there's nothing my God cannot do!" That's a good reminder for all of God's people today. God is able and available to tackle the seemingly impossible obstacle that is in front of you today. Is your problem financial, physical, emotional, interpersonal or spiritual? In Christ is the reservoir of mighty power. And that power is only accessed by faith.

Faith is how we *activate* God's power. Jesus said, "I tell you the truth, if you have faith as small as a mustard seed, you can say to this mountain, 'Move from here to there' and it will move. Nothing will be impossible for you" (Matthew 17:20). It's not that our faith makes *us* strong, but that our faith concedes our weakness and relies on God's strength instead. There are some things that God may only do when we stop struggling and start trusting. Stop and tell God you believe nothing is impossible for Him.

Faith is also how we *accept* God's response. We don't trust God simply to get something from God, like putting a token into a vending machine. Faith is our abiding confidence in God to be God. He has the prerogative to do as He sees fit and we will trust Him no matter the outcome.

Robert Louis Stevenson relates the story of passengers on a steamship that was caught in the middle of a severe storm. They began to whisper among themselves, "Is it safe? Are we going to sink?" One passenger set out to find some assurance and made his way topside, across the heaving decks, to the pilot house. The captain, his hand firmly on the wheel, saw the fear in the passenger's face and smiled, not speaking a word. The passenger made his way back below and exclaimed to the others, "We're going to be all right! I've seen the face of the pilot and he smiled at me."

When you are hit by stormy waves and crippling fear overtakes you, you can look into the peaceful face of Jesus, the Captain of your life. He has His hand on the wheel and you can have confidence that He is in full control. Faith is not only trusting in God to do something, but also accepting God's sovereign response. Turn to Jesus who is Mighty God, and Mighty God *for you!*

# DAY 21
# THE WONDER OF OUR EVERLASTING FATHER

*And he will be called...Everlasting Father.* —Isaiah 9:6

In the previous chapters, we have been looking at Isaiah 9:6, one of the most Christmas-centric prophecies in the Old Testament. It is not too much for us to think of Jesus as a "Wonderful Counselor" or "Mighty God. But what does the reader make of calling the "child to be born to us" our "Everlasting Father"? The title feels a bit like the riddle: "Brothers and sisters have I none. That man's father is my father's son." What does it mean that Jesus, the Son of God, is our "Father of all eternity"? The answer is found in His heavenly identity and His earthly ministry.

First notice that the title "Everlasting Father" connects Jesus in the Trinity. This crucial, historic doctrine of the Christian faith is one of the most difficult theological concepts to comprehend. It declares that the Father, the Son, and the Holy Spirit are co-equal in nature, but distinct in their persons. What is true of one is true of all three. So, while Jesus is not the Father or the Spirit, He shares all the same attributes. In John 14:9-10, Jesus said, "Anyone who has seen me has seen the Father" and "I am in the Father and the Father is in me." Jesus wasn't saying that He *is* the Father, but that what is in God the Father is also in Him and vice versa. Again, in John 10:30 He affirmed, "I and the Father are one."

This isn't mere theological reflection. It means that the eternal God came to us. Seeing our desperate need to be rescued from sin, God didn't dispatch an archangel or some earthly hero-warrior. God came personally to deal decisively with our problem and provide a way back to Him. In 1738, Charles Wesley penned the wonder of this great truth in his hymn "And Can It Be,"

*And can it be that I should gain*
*An int'rest in the Savior's blood?*
*Died He for me, who caused His pain?*
*For me, who Him to death pursued?*
*Amazing love! how can it be*
*That Thou, my God, should die for me?*

## A GOOD, GOOD FATHER

Calling Jesus our "Everlasting Father" doesn't end there, however. The title also anticipates His loving ministry. The Jews would not have usually referred to God as "Father." The fatherhood of God appears in the Old Testament, but not frequently. So, when Jesus began His model prayer with "Our Father in heaven" (Matthew 6:9), it would have caught the attention of His hearers. This fatherliness helps us to appreciate how Jesus relates to us.

For example, just as a father has compassion on the difficulties facing their children (Psalm 103:13), so Jesus was moved with compassion when He saw the needs of crowds and individuals (Mark 6:34, Matthew 20:34). After healing a woman of her bleeding, Jesus even referred to her as "daughter" (Mark 5:34) and, raising a little girl from the dead, He called her "my child" (Luke 8:54). Jesus feels the depth of hurt we feel. Like a father, he longs for us to be whole.

Similarly, just as a father teaches His children, so Jesus came to show us the truth (John 14:6). Everywhere He travelled, Jesus taught the crowds and amazed many with His teaching. Because Christ is the "treasure of all wisdom and knowledge" (Colossians 2:3), He offers us practical insight on how to live with God and one another.

Also, like a father is patient with his children, so Jesus deals patiently with people. We see His patience with the woman at the well who had multiple marriages, with the fearful disciples struggling at the oars in a violent storm on the sea, with Peter lopping off the ear of a servant in the Garden of Gethsemane, and with the failure of many to believe that He had been raised from the dead. Rather than grow exasperated, Jesus bore with great patience the ignorance, faithlessness, impulsiveness and fears of people. He still does.

Like a father, Jesus sacrificed Himself for His children. All earthly fathers would gladly trade their life to ease the suffering of their children. In the same way, Jesus took on our failure and sin and bore the brunt of justice so that we could live. He did not come to be served, but to serve and to give His life as a ransom for many (Mark 10:45).

Finally, like every good father, Jesus defends His children. He knows that we are bullied by the enemy throughout life and He is ready to come to our rescue. Because Jesus is eternal—without beginning or end—He guarantees His people life beyond death, not a vacant annihilation as some suggest. And, because He lives forever, Jesus sits at the Father's right-hand advocating for His people as their Great High Priest (Hebrews 7:25). John writes, "My dear children, I write this to you so that you will not sin. But if anybody does sin, we have one who speaks to the Father in our defense—Jesus Christ, the Righteous One" (1 John 2:1).

The chorus of a contemporary worship song declares, "You're a good, good Father. Yes, You are, yes You are." We know that God the Father is good to us because of what God the Son did in His ministry. Jesus proves that He is our Everlasting Father in loving us like a good father does.

# DAY 22
# THE WONDER OF OUR PRINCE OF PEACE

*And he will be called...Prince of Peace.* —Isaiah 9:6

After the birth of their fifth child, a couple received a playpen from some friends. Several weeks later, a thank you note arrived in the mail from the new mother. It read, "The playpen is wonderful. Just what I needed. I sit in it every afternoon and read for an hour. Without five kids hanging all over me, I'm finally able to get a little peace and quiet."

That would be nice.

In the last 4000 years, there have been fewer than 300 years of world "peace and quiet" and never more than four consecutive years in a row. Even as I write this entry, Israelis and Palestinians are once again at war, launching daily rocket attacks into each other's cities. Our nation has experienced an exponential increase in political polarization, racial unrest and ideological division. In 2021, the United States averaged more than one mass shooting per day. Instances of depression, self-harm and suicide continue to rise, especially among teenagers. Conflict is a never-ending reality—globally, domestically and personally.

Not surprisingly, with the convergence of a worldwide pandemic, political rhetoric and record unemployment, the most frequently searched topics in the YouVersion Bible App in 2020 were "fear" and "anxiety." Founder Bobby Gruenewald said,

"Through every hardship, people continue to seek God and turn to the Bible for strength, peace, and hope." This was as much true for the recipients of Isaiah's prophecy thousands of years ago as it is today. Surrounded by conflict on every side, God promised a Savior, then and now, who will be called our Prince of Peace (Isaiah 6:9).

## I COME IN PEACE

Peacemaking was the centerpiece of Jesus' ministry. That's why His birth announcement, sung by a heavenly choir, proclaimed "Glory to God in the highest, and on earth *peace to men* on whom his favor rests" (Luke 2:14). Jesus' arrived on a mission of peace. He is the Captain—the Prince—of all peace.

The Hebrew word for peace, *shalom,* means more than the absence of conflict. It refers to the safety, flourishing and well-being of people. Where there is peace, we expect to find whole-

> **where there is peace, we expect to find wholeness, prosperity, health and harmony.**

ness, prosperity, health, and harmony. And, this is what Jesus offered those who trust in Him. In fact, as Jesus looked to His imminent death, He comforted His troubled disciples by saying, "Peace I leave with you; my peace I give you. I do not give to you as the world gives. Do not let your hearts be troubled and do not be afraid" (John 14:27). And His first words after His resurrection were "Peace be with you!" (John 20:19). Jesus is peace and there are three dimensions to the peace He brings.

Most importantly, Jesus secures *upward peace* for us. This is vertical peace with God. All people are born sinners, deserving of God's wrath. We are enemies, in perpetual conflict with our

Creator. Only Jesus can end this struggle through His death on the cross. He gave Himself to satisfy the demands of God's justice, and when a person trusts Jesus' sacrifice, they are put into a right relationship with God. Paul writes, "Therefore, since we have been justified through faith, we have peace with God through our Lord Jesus Christ" (Romans 5:1). Peace *with* God is found through faith in Jesus.

Second, Jesus secures *inward peace* for us. This is the internal contentment and gladness a person enjoys because they trust that God is at the helm of life. God's Word affirms, "You will keep in perfect peace him whose mind is steadfast, because he trusts in you" (Isaiah 26:3). When we know that God has set us free from sin, welcomes us without blame, and has secured for us a guaranteed eternity with him, we can rest in peace free from any earthly anxiety or concern. The transcendent peace of God perpetually guards our heart and mind in Christ Jesus (Philippians 4:6-7).

Duke University conducted a study on people who have a such a "peace of mind." They discovered several characteristics:

- An absence of suspicion and resentment. People at peace don't nurse grudges.
- Not living in the past. People at peace embrace forgiveness and aren't dragged down by old mistakes and failures.
- Refusal to waste time and energy fighting conditions they cannot change. They look forward in hope.
- Refusal to indulge in self-pity when life hands them a raw deal. People at peace aren't victims but optimistic conquerors.
- Ability to laugh at circumstances. People at peace can breathe because they know this life is passing.

- Compassion toward others. People at peace take the focus off themselves and are concerned for their neighbor's needs.
- Pursue something bigger than themselves. Knowing that God has set them free, they walk by faith to make a difference.

Finally, Jesus secures *outward peace* for us. Peace *with* God enables us to live peaceably with others. Grace begets grace. Paul writes that God has given every Christian a ministry of reconciliation (2 Corinthians 5:18-19). This means that forgiven and free people *can* and *must* be emissaries of heavenly peace in the world. Forgive your enemy, preach hope, announce the Good News of the Kingdom, be the aroma of joy in every place. Bring peace to everyone, everywhere, because the peace of God rules in your soul. "If it is possible, as far as it depends on you, live at peace with everyone" (Romans 12:18).

The peace and quiet you're seeking is found in Jesus, the Prince of Peace. Bring Him your burdens and anxieties—the battle inside and outside. Let Him handle your hardest problem and restore your most difficult relationships. He has made a way for the wars to cease between you and God. Continue to trust Him in your relationships with others. And trust Him to settle your heart in shalom because you know Him and you know He cares for you.

# DAY 23
# THE WONDER OF LOVE

*This is how God showed his love among us: He sent his one and only Son into the world that we might live through him.* —1 John 4:9

Author Candy Chand shares a powerful story in her little book *Christmas Love.* One Christmas, she struggled to find the true meaning of the celebration. Her son, Nicholas, was in kindergarten and had been memorizing songs for his school's "Winter Pageant." Because the public school had stopped making any reference to "Christmas," she expected nothing more than a commercialized presentation of reindeer, Santa Claus, snowflakes, and good cheer. So, Chand was surprised when Nicholas and his class bounded up to the stage to perform their song "Christmas Love."

The class was dressed in their mittens, red sweaters, and holiday snow caps. As they sang, children in the front row held up large letters to spell out the title of the song. As they sang "C is for Christmas," a child held up the letter C. Then, "H is for Happy" and a child held up the letter H. Each verse of the song coordinated with one of the letters. All was going smoothly until the little girl holding the "M" turned the letter upside down. She was unaware of her mistake, though the 1st through 6th graders snickered at the gaffe. The song continued, her blunder on display until the end.

Then the room grew quiet.

As the kindergarteners finished their production, all the letter-holders proudly lifted their cardboard initials in the air and there it was: CHRIST**WAS** LOVE. The message was loud and clear.

The wonder of Christmas is that it is a love story. Over and again, the Bible affirms God's gracious love for humanity as a motivating factor for giving the gift of His Son:

> "The Lord your God is with you, he is mighty to save. He will take great delight in you, he will quiet you with his love, he will rejoice over you with singing." (Zephaniah 3:17)

> "For God so loved the world that he gave his one and only Son, that whoever believes in him shall not perish but have eternal life." (John 3:16)

> "This is how God showed his love among us: He sent his one and only Son into the world that we might live through him. This is love: not that we loved God, but that he loved us and sent his Son as an atoning sacrifice for our sins." (1 John 4:9-10)

> "But God demonstrates his own love for us in this: While we were still sinners, Christ died for us." (Romans 5:8)

Love is who God is and what God does. It is in His nature to love people, and Jesus is the proof of His love. But how? Just as it's easy to see when a young man is in love with a girl, so it is easy to read the story of Jesus and see exactly how God proved His love for each one of us. Consider the following:

**Love Pursues.** When one person loves another, they run after them, court them, and do their best to win them over. They're not satisfied to sit back and wait for the other to come to their senses. They launch a pursuit. This is what God did for us. Left to ourselves, we could have never found God by ourselves. So He found us. God left His throne in heaven and proved His love by chasing down unworthy sinners to make us His children. In the parables of the Lost Sheep and the Prodigal Son (Luke 15), Jesus highlights this pursuing love in the shepherd who leaves 99 lambs to find one wayward one and the father who saw his rebellious son "from a long way off" and graciously welcomed him home. God didn't wait for us to come to Him; He loved us enough to come to us.

**Love Sacrifices.** Most jewelers say that a diamond is worth "whatever someone is willing to pay for it." In other words, very few diamonds have any genuine worth except for the amount a lover is prepared to pay for his or her beloved. We prove our love for one another through sacrifice — gemstones, flowers, fine restaurants, and luxury vacations. God proves His love for us through extravagant sacrifice: the gift of His only Son. Jesus said, "Greater love has no one than this, that he lay down his life for his friends" (John 15:13).

**Love Endures.** As Paul completes his list of love-qualities, he writes "Love never fails" (1 Corinthians 13:8). We have fewer and fewer examples of this kind of enduring love in our world today. So we may not be able to fully comprehend God who will never leave us or forsake us. God will never love you more than He does today and He'll never love you less. Read Romans 8:37-39 to remember than nothing can separate us from the love of God that is found in Jesus!

## YOU ARE LOVED

In her memoir, *The Whisper Test*, Mary Ann Bird recounts the beautiful story of her path to life transformation. She writes,

I grew up knowing I was different, and I hated it. I was born with a cleft palate, and when I started school, my classmates made it clear to me how I looked to others: a little girl with a misshapen lip, crooked nose, lopsided teeth, and garbled speech. When schoolmates asked, "What happened to your lip?" I'd tell them I'd fallen and cut it on a piece of glass. Somehow it seemed more acceptable to have suffered an accident than to have been born different. I was convinced that no one outside my family could love me. There was, however, a teacher in the second grade whom we all adored. Her name was Mrs. Leonard. She was a short, round, happy, sparkling lady. Every year we had a hearing test. Mrs. Leonard gave the test to everyone in the class, and one year I went last. I knew from past years that as we stood against the door and covered one ear, the teacher sitting at her desk would whisper something, and we would have to repeat it back — things like "The sky is blue" or "Do you have new shoes?" I waited there and listened and heard words that God must have put into her mouth, seven words that changed my life. Mrs. Leonard said, in her whisper, "I wish you were my little girl."

Bird recalls how those seven simple words brought her out of her shell and restored her confidence. She was loved and that was enough. As misshapen as we are, God loves us. His great love isn't mere sentimentality but personal and life-changing. The message of Christmas is this: Christ Was Love!

# DAY 24
# THE WONDER OF IMMANUEL

*The virgin will be with child and will give birth to a son, and they will call him Immanuel—which means, "God with us."* —Matthew 1:23

In the Christian church calendar, the season that includes the four Sundays leading up to Christmas is referred to as Advent. The word means "the coming arrival of something or someone that is important or worthy of note." When we speak of the advent of the printing press or the advent of air conditioning or the advent of liberalism, we mean the emergence of something that had not been experienced previously. The arrival of such things changes everything else.

Christmas celebrates the advent of Christ—not just the miracle that Jesus was born, but the magnificent arrival of God come to earth. When Matthew writes of the heavenly conception of Mary, he notes that it fulfilled what the Lord had prophesied 800 years prior: "The virgin will be with child and will give birth to a son, and they will call him Immanuel—which means, 'God with us'" (Matthew 1:23, Isaiah 7:14).

Let that sink in for a moment. God. With. Us.

## ABOVE, AROUND, AGAINST, AMONG

It's not too much to think of God *above* us. He is the God "who is in heaven" and rules with rightful authority from there.

Satan tried to assert himself over God (see Isaiah 14:13) but was brought low to the pit because nothing is above the Almighty. As Solomon dedicated the temple, he exclaimed about God, "The heavens, even the highest heaven, cannot contain you" (1 Kings 8:27). Likewise, the psalmist declared, "The LORD is exalted over all the nations, His glory above the heavens. Who is like the LORD our God, the One who sits enthroned on high, who stoops down to look on the heavens and the earth?" (Psalm 113:4-6).

It's also not too much to think of God *around* us. God is omnipresent—everywhere, not limited to space or time. David is contented by the fact, "If I go up to the heavens, you are there; if I make my bed in the depths, you are there" (Psalm 139:8). The glory of God is evident in all His creation (Psalm 19:1) and He is ever-present holding all things together by His mighty power (Colossians 1:17). God is all around us, all the time.

It's also not too much to think of God *against* us. It's not a comforting thought, but our sin separates us from God (Isaiah 59:2, Romans 6:23) and makes Him hide His holy face from our iniquities. As sinners, we are rebels and enemies of God so it is not surprising that He would stand opposed to us. The face of the Lord is against those who do evil (1 Peter 3:12).

So, we believe God may be above us, around us and against us. But it is quite *un*believable to learn that God has come to live *among* us. But that's exactly what the advent of Christ means. God came near. The high and exalted One descended from the heavens to earth. The infinite One became tangible and touchable. The offended One became a close friend.

This sets our true God apart from other so-called gods in history. Moses said, "What other nation is so great as to have their gods near them the way the LORD our God is near us whenever we pray to him?" (Deuteronomy 4:7). God has always made Himself accessible to His people. But Christmas celebrates God

# we believe god may be above us, around us, and against us. But it is quite *un*believable to learn that god has come to live *among* us.

who came personally to be like us, serve us, empathize with us and save us.

Take a moment and consider the limitations God assumed to come live among us. God limited Himself in time and space. When Jesus visited Capernaum, He was not in Caesarea. He endured the restrictions of ordinary matter, not the liberty of omnipresence. And this self-limitation required that Jesus grow and eat and sleep and eventually bleed.

Second, God limited His glory. Though Jesus was God, He didn't flaunt His dazzling glory (Philippians 2:5). For a brief moment, He put His magnificence on display for His disciples (Mark 9:2-3), but most of the time, Jesus was ordinary enough that He was mistaken, misunderstood and mistreated. Very few people thought He was God in their midst.

Third, God limited His justice. How many times was Jesus abused, ignored, betrayed or offended? At any time, He could have executed His righteous judgment. But, instead, He "bit His tongue" (Isaiah 53:7) and held back His hand of wrath. What patience, what mercy, what self-control!

Ultimately, God limited His freedom. God is the sovereign authority over the whole universe. He bows to no one. But, from the moment He was tightly swaddled, all the way to His arrest, trials and crucifixion, Jesus was constrained, surrendering Himself to earthly authorities. He willingly gave up His freedom to set us free.

That God would limit Himself confounds all human understanding. Why on earth would He limit Himself, His glory, His justice and His freedom? The answer is simply: Love. God so loved the world that He came here. The greatest gift God gave at Christmas was the gift of Himself. In Christ, the King left His home, clothed Himself in our flesh, ate our food, endured our suffering and died our death so that He could give us *His* life. God has come to you so that you might come to God. The Son of God became a son of man so that the children of men could become children of God. He limited Himself so that we might discover limitless joy. Psalm 15:11 announces:

> But let all who take refuge in you be glad;
>     let them ever sing for joy.
> Spread your protection over them,
>     that those who love your name may rejoice in you!

# THE WONDER OF JESUS

*Mary...will give birth to a son, and you are to give him the name Jesus, because he will save his people from their sins.* —Matthew 1:20-21

The names of my grandchildren were a closely guarded secret by their parents until the babies were born. Then, at the hospital, my son handed me a little bundle and said "Dad, meet June." I was overwhelmed. Two years later, the announcement came via telephone, "His name is Otto David"—a grandson and my namesake. All at once, these pregnancies received identities. They became little people making history and possessing a destiny. Since those birthdays, both children have continued to grow into their names. They are becoming exactly what we expect a "June" and an "Otto" to be.

When the angel announced the miraculous conception of Christ, the Christmas baby's name was no secret. Joseph was told, "Mary...will give birth to a son, and you are to give him the name Jesus, because he will save his people from their sins" (Matthew 1:20-21).

Call Him "Jesus."

This given name was quite common in ancient Israel. Archeologists have located the tombs of more than 70 people with the name "Jesus" from this time period. Just as the name "Michael" has been the most popular name in the United States during 44 of the last 100 years, Jesus might well have been named Mike if

117

He was born today. Still, as common as it may have been, Jesus' name fit Him better than any other Jesus before or after.

His name means "The Lord saves." Throughout the Old Testament, Israel looked for and longed for the day of God's rescue. Facing imminent threat from their enemies, Jeremiah prophesied,

> "The days are coming," declares the Lord,
>   "when I will raise up to David a righteous Branch,
> a King who will reign wisely
>   and do what is just and right in the land.
> In his days Judah will be saved
>   and Israel will live in safety.
> This is the name by which he will be called:
>   The Lord Our Righteousness." (Jeremiah 23:5-6)

Jesus is the Branch from the family tree of David. He is the reigning King from heaven. He is the righteous Lord. He is God who has come to rescue Judah and Israel and everyone else. His name is His mission: God saves!

## JOSHUA TO JESUS

To better understand Jesus' rescuing ministry, let's look back at another "Jesus" in the past. Joshua in Hebrew means the same thing as Jesus in Greek. Joshua is a shadow of Jesus in the Old Testament, and the New Testament writers regard him as such. As the Israelites fled Egypt, initially under Moses' guidance, Joshua was appointed to bring God's people home. Under his leadership, the people of God were saved from, through and for something.

First, God's people were saved *from* their Egyptian enemies and the desperate wilderness wandering that followed. Joshua was used by God to lead people out of an oppressive, hopeless past and into a new future with God. In the same way, Jesus came to rescue people from the dominion of darkness (1 Peter 2:9). Sin, Satan and death is the enemy of every person and Jesus came to save us from all three. Through His death on the cross, our sin may be forgiven and, through His resurrection from the dead, our victory over the devil and our resurrection from the dead is guaranteed. Through Jesus, God has saved us from our past.

God also saves us *through* our present circumstances. As the people of God approached the land of Canaan, the Jordan River blocked their easy passage home. But, reminiscent of Moses at the Red Sea crossing, Joshua stepped into the surging river, the waters stopped upstream, and the multitudes crossed over on dry ground. Similarly, the Christian faces seemingly uncrossable obstacles in this life—temptation, suffering, pressure and persecution. But Jesus has gone before us, stepping into the stream and showing us the way through. He leads us to victory and endurance and peace and steadfastness of hope (Philippians 4:13).

Ultimately, God rescues us *for* life with Him. Just as Joshua led the Israelites from the wilderness, through the river and into the promised land, so Jesus leads us out of sin and death, through the struggles of this life and finally into the promised land of the Kingdom of God. Hebrews 4:8 states that if the people of God had received their final rest simply by inheriting Canaan, Joshua would not have spoken about another, better rest in the future. God did not save people for life here, but a home with Him forever (John 14:1-4).

This Christmas, celebrate the wonder of Jesus. His name reveals His necessity. In Jesus Christ, God completes His rescue mission in the world. Through the birth of His Son, God has saved us from the past, saves us through our present circumstances and saves us for eternity with Him. Merry Christmas!

# DAY 26
# THE WONDER OF A WELCOME

*When King Herod heard this he was disturbed, and all Jerusalem with him.* —Matthew 2:3

**M**ore than once, I've heard the impassioned outcry among Christians: "Don't let them take Christ out of Christmas!" The protest is often incited by an advertisement featuring "Xmas"—an ugly "X" stamping out the name of Christ. Never mind that the first use of "Xmas" dates to the 17th Century and was used predominately *in the church*. The Greek letter Chi ("X") has historically been used as a symbol for Christ. And the Chi Rho is one of the earliest Christograms, dating to 300 A.D. So, "Xmas" was never intended to mark out the reason for the season.

Nonetheless, Jesus hasn't been warmly welcomed by everyone. The announcement of His birth was met with a mixed reception among those who heard it. Matthew 2:1-12 records the responses from three types of people.

King Herod represents the *Antagonists*. Serving under Caesar Augustus as the ruler over Judea, Herod was about 70 years old when Jesus was born. His business card title was "King of the Jews," so when foreigners arrived in Jerusalem asking about "the one born king of the Jews," Herod became "disturbed" (v. 3). Matthew adds that all the citizens of Jerusalem followed suit in his concern because, if Herod is unsettled, everyone pays a price.

His little kingdom threatened, Herod launched a defensive attack by seeking out his newborn rival and eventually killing children throughout Bethlehem to neutralize his competition.

Herod wouldn't be the last hater to come against Jesus. Frequently, the religious elite challenged Jesus and tried to sideline His mission. Fueled by pride, jealousy and mistrust, they rejected Jesus' message and ministry and conspired to lead others away from Him. More than once, Jesus warned His disciples that He would "suffer many things at the hands of the elders, chief priests and teachers of the law, and that he must be killed and on the third day be raised to life" (Matthew 16:21, Mark 8:31).

Such antagonism continues today. Many in the world are opposed to Jesus, their little kingdoms threatened by His claim to be the only sovereign King. That Jesus claims to be the exclusive "way, the truth and the life" scandalizes human freedom, opinion and individualism. How dare He call anyone to repent and follow Him alone! Even mentioning the name of Jesus can raise the temperature of public discourse. It is not too much to say that there have always been—and still are—those who hate Jesus (John 15:18).

## WHO CARES?

A second group of people are the *Ambivalents*, represented by the religious experts whom Herod summoned to learn more about the Jewish Messiah. When asked about where such a king was to be born, they answered, "In Bethlehem in Judea, for this is what the prophet has written" (v. 5). They quoted the chapter and verse prophecy from Micah 5:2 but ultimately did nothing. The arrival of the long-awaited Savior of Israel should have stirred their hearts with excitement and expectation. But they shrugged their shoulders with indifference.

Unfortunately, religious ambivalence is common among people today. Theological liberalism has stripped Jesus of all divinity and wonder, leaving a bare-bones skeleton of a "nice teacher." Religious pluralism has reduced Jesus to one of many options that people can choose on the buffet of personal preference. And Christian nominalism has made following Jesus nothing more than a gym membership with few committed members. While the Antagonists push to "X" Jesus out of Christmas and everything else, the Ambivalents wouldn't notice if it happened or not. They just don't care.

## COME LET US ADORE HIM!

The remaining group—the *Adorers*—are represented by the Magi who made their way to welcome and worship the King. They left their home in the east and travelled to Jerusalem and beyond to find Jesus. When they found the baby—probably about two years old by this time—they "bowed down and worshipped Him" (v. 11). Two actions reflected their adoration of King Jesus.

First, they "bowed down." Bowing is a universal posture of humility. In lowering oneself, a person makes another higher, greater. We adore Jesus sometimes by literally bowing, kneeling or laying prostrate on our face in worship. But bowing is ultimately a heart disposition. It is declaring that Jesus is the rightful King over me and gladly surrendering everything I have to Him and His purposes. We bow when we say to Jesus, "Take my life, my money, my possessions, my children, my time, my future. It's all Yours and I willingly give you control over everything. You are my King and I am your humble servant." That's adoration.

Second, they "worshipped." Since he has already mentioned "bowing," Matthew must mean more than simply paying homage to Jesus. Their worship was reflected in their sacrifice. They opened their treasure boxes and gave Jesus gifts of gold, frankincense and myrrh. Today, we worship Jesus through sacrifice. Surrender means that we give freely; sacrifice means that we give generously. Like David who chose to worship at great personal cost, sacrifice means that we "will not offer burnt offerings to the Lord my God that cost me nothing" (2 Samuel 24:24).

What kind of welcome does Jesus get from you? Antagonism, ambivalence or adoration? Take a moment, bow, and worship. Consider what surrender and sacrifice you will offer to your King.

*O come, all ye faithful, joyful and triumphant!*
*O come ye, O come ye to Bethlehem;*
*Come and behold Him*
*Born the King of angels:*
*O come, let us adore Him,*
*Christ the Lord.*

# DAY 27
# THE WONDER OF TREASURE

*Sovereign Lord, as you have promised, you now dismiss your servant in peace.* —Luke 2:29

Everyone should have a bucket list. This is the short list of experiences and expectations a person dreams about enjoying before they "kick the bucket." Not surprisingly, the older I get, the fewer items remain on my bucket list. Travel to Africa and India, check. Skydive, check. Get my doctorate, check. Write a book, check. One friend warned me that I shouldn't complete my list too quickly as a completed bucket list meant death was imminently around the corner.

At Christmas we meet a man who had a bucket list. Simeon was a devout Jew who had been "waiting for the consolation of Israel" (Luke 2:25)—the coming comfort of a Messiah who would restore God's people. The Holy Spirit had revealed to Simeon that he wouldn't die until he had seen the fulfillment of this promise. So, this aging saint held tightly to his one-item bucket list.

Simeon was in the temple court one day, perhaps oblivious to the usual activity of worshippers coming and going, daily sacrifices, and the noisy din of money being exchanged and animals traded. Suddenly, his eye caught sight of a young peasant girl and her husband. They were unspectacular among the crowd that day. And, they had come to fulfill the Law by consecrating their infant son 40 days after his birth. Offering their modest sacrifice of two doves, the couple turned to leave the temple when Simeon interrupted.

"Excuse me, may I see your child?"

No doubt, Mary and Joseph had been asked the question before. Children were a cherished gift in Israel, and who wouldn't want to see a tangible expression of God's blessing? Even today, it's not uncommon for a stranger to pay a passing compliment about another's newborn.

But this was different. Simeon took the infant in his arms and praised God, saying:

> "Sovereign Lord, as you have promised,
>     you now dismiss your servant in peace.
> For my eyes have seen your salvation,
>     which you have prepared in the sight of all people,
> a light for revelation to the Gentiles
>     and for glory to your people Israel." (Luke 2:29-32)

Simeon's short song has classically been called the *Nunc Dimittus*—Latin for "Now Dismiss." Holding the Savior close to his heart, Simeon cried out, "Take me home, God! I can die a happy man! I have met Your peace sent to the world and now I am at peace. My bucket list is complete!"

## NOW DISMISS

Simeon's story teaches us that Christ is found by those who seek Him. It was not enough that the Spirit assured the old man that he would one day see the Messiah. Simeon set about searching, keeping his eyes and his heart open. This is the pattern of others in the Christmas story. The Magi in the east saw a great star and followed it to the place where the baby lay. The shepherds heard the heavenly chorus and went to Bethlehem to see what God was doing. People found Christ when they took time to look for Christ.

God has sent us a precious gift in Jesus Christ. He is a gift worth searching for. And the Bible assures us that He will be found by those who search. The promise found in the Old Covenant ("You will seek me and find me when you seek me with all your heart"—Jeremiah 29:13) is repeated in the New Covenant ("Ask and it will be given to you; seek and you will find; knock

| God has sent us a precious gift in Jesus christ. He is a gift worth searching for. And the Bible assures us that He will be found by those who search.

and the door will be opened to you. For everyone who asks receives; he who seeks finds; and to him who knocks, the door will be opened"—Matthew 7:7-8). God does not wish to remain hidden. He is discovered by those who seek.

Simeon's story also reminds us that once we've seen God's salvation, we can die in peace. When I was a child, I begged my parents for a 10-speed bicycle, a BB gun, or a stereo for Christmas. I guaranteed them that, if I got what I wanted, I would be "the happiest kid on earth." It never worked.

Because nothing but Jesus brings peace.

When Simeon held Christ, he discovered a gladness that nothing else on earth can bring. Hold Christ close to your heart, enter into an abiding relationship with Him, and both your living and your dying are contented. Nothing else compares to the eternal treasure we gain in Him. Saint Augustine wrote, "Thou hast made us for Thyself and our hearts are restless until they find their rest in Thee."

Only one item is necessary on your bucket list of life: Find Jesus. Seek Him and savor Him every day. Having peace with Jesus, you will be able to come to the end of life and say to God, "Now Dismiss" —I have found my greatest treasure.

# DAY 28
# THE WONDER OF A KINGDOM

*He will reign on David's throne and over his kingdom, establishing and upholding it with justice and righteousness...* —Isaiah 9:7

Two weeks after the assassination of her husband, Jackie Kennedy gave an interview to *Life* magazine. One of the most memorable lines in her story read, "There will be great presidents again, but there will never be another Camelot." Mrs. Kennedy was referring to JFK's love for the King Arthur legend and compared his presidency to the idyllic, romantic, heroic kingdom. A British historian in the 12th century described Arthur as "a warrior and leader of almost supernatural capacity, and also a youth of such unparalleled courage and generosity, joined with that sweetness of temper and innate goodness, as gained him universal love."

Of course, Camelot was mere myth. And Kennedy's presidency was only as good as one's political affinity. Fortunately, there *is* a kingdom better than medieval lore or party platforms. It's the Kingdom of God. And Christmas is the advent of His kingdom.

Seven hundred years before the birth of Jesus, Isaiah anticipated the earthly realm of God's reign. He prophesied, "A shoot will come up from the stump of Jesse; from his roots a Branch will bear fruit" (Isaiah 11:1). Jesse was David's father and from David's line came a long list of kings who ruled over Israel and

Judah. Very few of the kings were good or godly and, subsequently, Israel was led into captivity in Assyria while Judah would be carted off to Babylon. God's people were subjects of kingdoms that were not their own. However, God promised to bring forth a shoot—a living branch that would bear fruit in a barren place.

Jesus is the descendant of David, our long-expected King. From the start of His ministry, Jesus campaigned "The Kingdom of heaven is near!" (Matthew 4:17). Later, He announced "the Kingdom of God is within (or among) you" (Luke 17:21). However, though the Kingdom was *inaugurated* at Jesus' first coming, it will not be *consummated* until He comes again. In other words, we still pray "Thy Kingdom come" (Matthew 6:10) every day. And, until God's Kingdom finally comes on earth as it is in heaven, Christians must live as exiles—first Kingdom people in a second kingdom place. Jesus, our King, teaches us what this kind of living looks like.

It starts with setting our sights on God. Isaiah writes that the Spirit of the Lord rested on Jesus and gave Him wisdom, understanding, counsel and power so that He delighted in the fear of the Lord (Isaiah 11:2-3). In other words, Jesus didn't live to please people or please Himself. He lived to please God. He was motivated by the Spirit of God to have the heart of God to do the things of God for the glory of God.

To live as Kingdom citizens now, Christians "set their mind" and "set their heart" on things above, where "Christ is seated at the right hand of God" (Colossians 3:1-2). They focus on God's priorities. They surrender to God's plans. They endeavor for God to be made famous through them. Bottom line: they want what God wants. Fortunately, the Holy Spirit who lives in the Christian is singularly God-focused and *eagerly wants* to help us please

God at every turn. So, hearing and heeding that spiritual prompt is what it means to live as Kingdom people.

Another aspect of Kingdom living is treating others justly. Isaiah describes the life of the King: "with righteousness, he will judge the needy, with justice He will give decisions for the poor of the earth" (Isaiah 11:4). "Justice" is simply doing what's right for people. In the Bible, it's a social/ethical concept, not merely a legal one. To act justly is to honor, advocate, liberate and defend people who might not be able to do so for themselves.

John the Baptist announced the arrival of Jesus and His Kingdom. But later, when he was arrested, John wondered whether Jesus was really the promised Messiah-King. So, he asked, "Are you the one who was to come, or should we expect someone else?" (Matthew 11:3). Jesus answered, "The blind receive sight, the lame walk, those who have leprosy are cured, the deaf hear, the dead are raised, and the good news is preached to the poor" (v. 5). Justice is the unmistakable evidence of the Kingdom of God. So, if you see justice, you are witnessing the Kingdom of heaven breaking into the kingdom of earth. Similarly, when Jesus' followers act with justice in their world—fighting for the life of the unborn, helping the immigrant and refugee, liberating teens from sex-trafficking, supporting religious liberty, actively working toward racial reconciliation, advocating for the homeless and poor, serving people with mental and physical limitations, or rescuing women from oppression, just to name a few— they prove their Kingdom identity.

Pause and ask yourself, "Who are the 'poor' around me? How might I leverage my position and resources to bring a blessing to others? Who needs a little extra help? What good thing can I do to manifest the greater goodness of God?" Then, ask the Lord to prepare an opportunity for you to act justly.

A final aspect of the Kingdom worth noting is the pursuit of universal peace. Isaiah writes,

> The wolf will live with the lamb, the leopard will lie down with the goat, the calf and the lion and the yearling together; and a little child will lead them. The cow will feed with the bear, their young will lie down together, and the lion will eat straw like the ox. The infant will play near the hole of the cobra, and the young child put his hand into the viper's nest. They will neither harm nor destroy on all my holy mountain, for the earth will be full of the knowledge of the Lord as the waters cover the sea. (Isaiah 11:6-9)

As mentioned earlier in this devotional, Jesus is the Prince of Peace who came to establish peace everywhere. When God's Kingdom comes, there will be no more need for prisons, vaccinations, Amber Alerts, crime scene tape, patriot funerals, marriage counselors, attorneys or automobile repair shops. Everything and everyone will be at rest—in perfect peace.

While global peace is only possible when Jesus comes, Christians can promote this peace in the meantime. Share the Gospel with a neighbor as a God's appointed minister of reconciliation (2 Corinthians 5:18). Shake off bitterness and forgive the person who has hurt you. Post words of hope rather than barbs of division on your social media feed. Hold your tongue when you know your comment won't change the course of the conversation. Resist being the devil's advocate. Paul commands, "Let us therefore make every effort to do what leads to peace and to mutual edification" (Romans 14:19). When we do, we prove our heavenly heritage (Matthew 5:9).

# DAY 29
# THE WONDER OF WAR

*The dragon stood in front of the woman who was about to give birth,*
*so that he might devour her child the moment it was born.*
*—Revelation 12:4*

In 1941, "The Little Drummer Boy" was introduced into our American Christmas tradition. He was an unexpected addition to the romanticized nativity setting with Joseph, Mary, the baby Jesus, cattle, sheep, shepherds, angels and wise men. The lyrics tell the story of a poor young boy who had been summoned by the Magi to visit the newborn king. Without any gift in hand, the kid played his little drum instead. Mary smiled, the ox and lamb swayed with the music, and a star was born.

Pa rum pum pum pum.

As nostalgic as the carol is, it does tease a spiritual reality. Jesus was born in wartime. As the child breathed in Bethlehem, an invasion was launched in a parallel universe. Battle lines were drawn as sinister forces of evil assembled their armies. At the infant's first cry, weapons of warfare were locked and loaded. Troops were ordered to the frontlines. And, if we close our eyes for a moment, we can imagine, in the hills of Bethlehem, the march of a little drummer boy. Maybe several. But they weren't making their way to the manger to entertain the King. They were marching, beating their drums, calling unseen forces to war!

This isn't the Christmas memory anyone expected. But it is most assuredly a picture of what was really going on at the birth of our Savior. Philip Yancey, in his *The Jesus I Never Knew*, confirms:

> There is [a] view of Christmas I have never seen on a Christmas card, probably because no artist, not even William Blake, could do it justice. Revelation 12 pulls back the curtain to give us a glimpse of Christmas as it must have looked from somewhere far beyond Andromeda: Christmas from the angels' viewpoint.

Indeed, Revelation 12 reveals a darker side of Christmas. While much of the chapter looks forward to the end time struggle when Jesus returns, two verses look back to the day Jesus was born. John writes,

> The dragon stood in front of the woman who was about to give birth, so that he might devour her child the moment it was born. She gave birth to a son, a male child, who will rule all the nations with an iron scepter. And her child was snatched up to God and to his throne. (Revelation 12:4-5)

To maintain consistency with the rest of the chapter, the "woman" in this passage is most likely the nation of Israel. The male "child" is Jesus, the "offspring" first announced in Genesis 3:15 and the promised "son" in Isaiah 7:14. The "dragon" is confirmed in verse nine to be Satan. So, while carolers sing sentiments like "Silent night, holy night, all is calm, all is bright..." and "O little town of Bethlehem, how still we see thee lie...," a cosmic conflict was unfolding in the birth pains of Mary. Locally, Herod crafted a conspiracy to kill his kingdom rival. But the rumors of war extended much beyond Israel. Satan had launched a rebellion in the Garden and was now bringing all his evil forces to bear in an attempt to thwart the redemptive plan of God.

The drumbeats of this war continue today.

## STILL AT WAR

Christians are warned to be on guard against the devil who "prowls around like a roaring lion looking for someone to devour" (1 Peter 5:8). We are commanded to put on all the armor of God so that we're able to stand against the enemy's schemes because "our struggle is not against flesh and blood, but against the rulers, against the authorities, against the powers of this dark world and against the spiritual forces of evil in the heavenly realms" (Ephesians 6:12). We hold our ground through confidence in what Jesus has done and in what Jesus will do.

Our confidence is strengthened because we can look back and see what Jesus has already accomplished. The devil gained no ground at Jesus' death. Through His crucifixion and His resurrection, Jesus secured for us freedom from the penalty and the power of sin. The Christian can be sure that the final battle has been already won! This is why Paul writes, "But thanks be to God! He gives us the victory through our Lord Jesus Christ!" (1 Corinthians 15:57) and "We are more than conquerors through him who loved us" (Romans 8:37). So, when we feel the pressures of this life—failure at work, sadness over the death of a spouse, the persistent struggle against temptation, the loss of a dream—don't let the drumming of war drown out trumpet blast of victory. Because Christ has won, you have won already! God loved you enough to send His Son who fought for you, died for you and rose again to secure your eternal freedom. Look back to help you look forward.

As we look ahead, our confidence is strengthened because of what we know Jesus will accomplish. On November 3, 1948, the *Chicago Daily Tribune* incorrectly printed the front page headline "Dewey Defeats Truman." Their premature announcement proved the danger in predicting an outcome. But, when we read our Bible, we can have unwavering confidence in the future triumph of Jesus Christ. The headline from Revelation 12:9 reads that the dragon "was hurled to the earth, and all his angels with him."

Jesus wins.

In the end, we don't stake our hope that the United States wins. Or capitalism wins. Or technology wins. Or exercise and body care wins. Or conservatism or liberalism wins. Or freedom wins. Or knowledge wins. All that matters is that the drumbeat in history will quicken, Jesus will return, and His victory will be swift and sure. The second verse of Luther's "A Mighty Fortress Is Our God" assures us that the end is written:

*Did we in our own strength confide,*
*our striving would be losing,*
*were not the right Man on our side,*
*the Man of God's own choosing.*
*You ask who that may be?*
*Christ Jesus, it is He;*
*Lord Sabaoth His name,*
*from age to age the same;*
*and He must win the battle.*

# DAY 30
# THE WONDER OF ESCAPE

*And so was fulfilled what the Lord had said through the prophet:*
*"Out of Egypt I called my son."* —Matthew 2:15

Christmas is beautiful, magical and hopeful. But wake up the day *after* Christmas and everything changes. The departure of the wise men crossfades into a declaration of war. Neither Herod's pride nor his politics could handle the birth of a truly Jewish king. So, he became the Scrooge of the real Christmas story and searched for Jesus to kill his rival. An angel tipped off Mary and Joseph to the assassination plan and directed them to escape to Egypt where they would hide until Herod's death (Matthew 2:13-15). The king, realizing that he had been duped by the foreign Magi, ordered the slaughter of all baby boys in Bethlehem and the surrounding vicinity. If he got lucky, he could still stay any threat to his throne.

The "Massacre of the Innocents" was prophesied hundreds of years prior (Hosea 11:1) and was reminiscent of Pharoah's extermination of the Hebrew boys just before the exodus (see Exodus 1:22). The enemy will continually create conflict with God's people and God's plans until Jesus returns. Even in the end times, kings of the earth will join forces with the antichrist and "They will make war against the Lamb, but the Lamb will overcome them because he is Lord of lords and King of kings—and with him will be his called, chosen and faithful followers" (Revelation 17:14). Just as the darkness of night wrestles to hold back the coming sun of dawn, so the devil wishes to prevent the rise of the Son of God. But Jesus will prevail just as the light of day always conquers the darkness of night.

## THE QUESTION EVERYONE IS ASKING

The escape of Jesus and His family raises a delicate question: Why didn't God rescue *all* the babies in Bethlehem? Matthew records,

Then what was said through the prophet Jeremiah was fulfilled:

"A voice is heard in Ramah,
    weeping and great mourning,
Rachel weeping for her children
    and refusing to be comforted
because they are no more." (Matthew 2:17-18)

Perhaps keeping to the shadows of the village as they fled, Mary and Joseph could hear the wails of grieving parents as Roman soldiers pushed their way into homes and put helpless babies to death at the sword. And while they would have no doubt been grateful for God's rescue of them, they might have wondered, "Why not everyone?" God knew the storm was coming. Why didn't He intervene?

This question rattles every soul whenever crisis strikes. Why doesn't God stop the suffering in the world? If He *knows* that people suffer…If He has the *power* to alleviate their suffering…If He *loves* people truly, why doesn't He rescue?

The question, though honest, forgets the source of all suffering. Our pain results from the lingering presence of sin. When Satan tempted Adam and Eve to abandon God's authority for their own autonomy, the resultant curse is that all of creation was contaminated by sin. Sin isn't just a moral condition. Sin damages our relationships, disrupts our climate, decomposes our body, degenerates our decency, destroys our systems, dements our mind, denies our truth, debases our values, defaces our beauty, derides our authorities, defiles our worship, devastates our success, deceives our reason, disables our progress and dismisses our God. The principle of sin has leeched into every dimension of life so that "the whole world is a prisoner of sin" (Galatians 3:22).

Now you can see the problem: For God to remove suffering, God must remove the source. If sin is the source of all suffering and sin is *in* us, then God must remove every last one of us to free the world of suffering. One writer said, "If we asked God to erase all pain at midnight tonight, who of us would be left at 12:01?" Perhaps God could have rescued all the babies in Bethle-

**For God to remove suffering, God must remove the source. If sin is the source of all suffering and sin is *in* us, then God must remove every last one of us to free the world of suffering.**

hem, but they would have lived to face suffering again and again and again. Because they were born into a sinful world.

This reality would make us utterly hopeless if it were not for God's ultimate salvation. God rescued the one baby who could rescue everyone else. As a child, Jesus escaped death, but would eventually die so that all the children who were destined to die could escape eternal death. You see, God did not ultimately send His Son to save us from the myriad of conflicts we face throughout life—arthritis, final exams, bankruptcy, blown transmissions, broken relationships, pinched nerves, an inoperable brain tumor, the loss of a beloved pet and much more. Jesus came to save us from an insufferable eternity separated from God because of the dark sin in our heart. Because Jesus has saved us eternally, we can face every conflict hopefully. Because of Him, we endure any present difficulty with confidence of our rescue still to come.

The wonder of escape is that God was saving His Son so that His Son could save us all.

# DAY 31
# THE WONDER OF RETURN

*"...the Son of Man will appear in the sky, and all the nations of the earth will mourn. They will see the Son of Man coming on the clouds of the sky, with power and great glory."* —Matthew 24:30

The visit of the President of the United States to a domestic or international city requires so much preparation. Streets are closed, airspace is restricted 30 minutes of his arrival, explosive detection canines have scouted every location, snipers are positioned in strategic vantage points and details of the executive itinerary are kept a closely guarded secret. Hundreds of personnel and weeks of planning ensure that travel, parades, banquets and personal appearances are in place for his arrival.

Contrast the coming of the most powerful leader in the world with the coming of the most powerful leader in the universe. More than 2000 years ago, there were no advance logistics teams, no motorcades, no welcome receptions or five-star hotels. Jesus was greeted by blue-collar shepherds and a few foreign astrologers before the holy family were sent running as refugees away from home. The first advent of Jesus was back page, below-the-fold news.

But His second coming will be much different!

The book of Revelation is the story of the final Christmas—a record of Jesus' return. And, if we look closely, we can see the continuity between both arrivals:

**EXPECTATION**—God's people today eagerly anticipate Jesus' return just as God's people throughout the Old Testament were looking forward to the Messiah.

**PREPARATION**—God is arranging historical events today to crescendo in His Son's return just as He was moving throughout history in the past so that Jesus would come at "just the right time."

**REJECTION**—In the times leading up to Jesus' return, the hearts of many people will grow cold, rejecting Jesus as Lord, just as many in Israel rejected Jesus as His first coming.

**VISITATION**—Just as God personally entered our world the first time, so Jesus will return personally, visibly and triumphantly again.

This future "Christmas" is described in Revelation 19. Leading up to this time, the antichrist has ascended to world dominance and initially appears to be sympathetic to Israel. His signature on a peace treaty commences a seven-year season of God's judgment marked by war, famine, fire, destruction, earthquakes, darkness and death. Two courageous witnesses rise up to preach to warn the world but are quickly martyred. Thousands of evangelists begin to preach the Gospel to Israel, which causes the antichrist to retract his treaty and force many to take his "mark" and worship him.

The stage is set. Evil seems to have prevailed. Perhaps all is lost.

And then, a trumpet blasts from heaven, loud enough for every creature alive to hear it. It's not a horn of entertainment, but a siren of imminent warfare. John writes:

I saw heaven standing open and there before me was a white horse, whose rider is called Faithful and True. With justice he judges and makes war. His eyes are like blazing fire, and on his head are many crowns. He has a name written on him that no one knows but he himself. He is dressed in a robe dipped in blood, and his name is the Word of God. The armies of heaven were following him, riding on white horses and dressed in fine linen, white and clean. Out of his mouth comes a sharp sword with which to strike down the nations. "He will rule them with an iron scepter." He treads the winepress of the fury of the wrath of God Almighty. On his robe and on his thigh he has this name written: KING OF KINGS AND LORD OF LORDS. (Revelation 19:11-16)

## GLORY, GLORY HALLELUJAH!

When Jesus came the first time He was cloaked in humility — a simple, unspectacular servant. But, at His second coming, the doors of heaven will be thrown off their hinges and the radiant glory of the Lord will be revealed in full display. In his vision, John saw Jesus in several portraits.

Jesus will come as a victorious Warrior. Jesus rode a donkey to His death the first time. But He will ride a white stallion at His triumphant return. As Jesus breathed His last on the cross, the sun was darkened, and it appeared that the devil had won the game. But our Savior rose from the dead and, for more than 2000 years, has been running toward a final victory. And, when Jesus comes, the "armies of heaven" — those who have trusted Jesus throughout history — will ride in their triumphal march with Him (2 Corinthians 2:14). For every person who experiences defeat, failure, frustration or loss, be hopeful. Jesus wins!

Jesus will come as a decisive Judge. His eyes, like blazing fire, survey every thought, intention, desire and action. Nothing slips by Him. What He sees He will judge according to the truth of His Word, the "sword of the Spirit" (Ephesians 6:17). And, in His righteous judgment, He will execute decisively. The scene that plays out in verses 17-21 isn't a pleasant one. It's a sober reminder that everyone is either God's friend or His enemy—in relationship or in rebellion. And, when He comes, Jesus will execute His final justice.

Jesus will come as a reigning King. Three miles southeast of Bethlehem stood King Herod's Herodium. Built on a high peak in the Judean desert, the edifice was the largest man-made structure at the time, sporting an indoor pool, a steam room and interior gardens. Jesus was born in the shadow of a palace fit for a king, but never honored by it. Today, Jesus is King, far above all "angels, authorities, and powers in submission to Him" (1 Peter 3:22). But His rightful authority is frequently eclipsed by governments, leaders, experts and rebels who refuse to submit to Him. When He comes, He will carry the royal scepter and will be crowned with many crowns. At that time, there will be no competition for His throne. Everyone will bow under the banner of the King of all kings.

In 1861, as the Civil War loomed over the United States, abolitionist poet Julia Ward Howe penned a battle cry that became popular among the Federal Army a year later. In the years since, "The Battle Hymn of the Republic" has been associated with fight for freedom. Forget that the song was sung on the battlefields of our nation and read the lyrics in the context of Jesus, our returning Warrior, Judge and King:

*Mine eyes have seen the glory of the coming of the Lord;*
*He is trampling out the vintage where the grapes of wrath are stored;*

*He hath loosed the fateful lightning of His terrible swift sword:*
*His truth is marching on.*

*I have seen Him in the watch-fires of a hundred circling camps,*
*They have builded Him an altar in the evening dews and damps;*
*I can read His righteous sentence by the dim and flaring lamps:*
*His day is marching on.*

*I have read a fiery gospel writ in burnished rows of steel:*
*"As ye deal with my contemners, so with you my grace shall deal";*
*Let the Hero, born of woman, crush the serpent with his heel,*
*Since God is marching on.*

*He has sounded forth the trumpet that shall never call retreat;*
*He is sifting out the hearts of men before His judgment-seat;*
*Oh, be swift, my soul, to answer Him! Be jubilant, my feet!*
*Our God is marching on.*

*In the beauty of the lilies Christ was born across the sea,*
*With a glory in His bosom that transfigures you and me.*
*As He died to make men holy, let us die to make men free,*
*While God is marching on.*

*Glory, glory, hallelujah!*
*Glory, glory, hallelujah!*
*Glory, glory, hallelujah!*
*Our God is marching on.*

How does one prepare for God who will one day march into history? Trust in Jesus who has guaranteed victory through His death and resurrection. Allow God's righteous wrath to fall on His Son rather than you. And start living under the banner of Jesus' reign every day. Glory, glory, hallelujah!

# CONCLUSION
# DO YOU STILL WONDER?

*Who among the gods is like you, O LORD? Who is like you—majestic in holiness, awesome in glory, working wonders?* —Exodus 15:11

This Advent journey was designed to woo your heart to wonder. Think back to the magnificence of prophecy, providence, faith, the Kingdom, worship, grace, wisdom, joy, love, salvation, hope and more. Each vignette reminds us that God has been at work in history, putting His glory on display so that people everywhere would stand speechless—in awe of their great God. After the Israelites had been rescued from the Egyptians in pursuit, Moses sang, "Who among the gods is like you, O LORD? Who is like you—majestic in holiness, awesome in glory, working wonders?" In other words, who can compare to our God who stands out in all of His wondrous glory?

Very soon, you will box up your Christmas decorations and store the lights and ornaments and nutcrackers in the attic until next year. Christmas is over and it's time to get on with life. Perhaps you might leave your Nativity scene out a little longer. What God did during the most wonderful time of the year should amaze our hearts in February, mid-July and when the leaves turn color next fall. The God who *was* at work is *still* at work and He wishes to capture your heart every day. How can you keep the wonder of Christmas going?

First, recall the lessons that you have learned along the way:

- The Gospel is God's gift to you, chosen long ago and un-wrapped in Jesus.
- God makes and keeps His promises to you.
- Prophecy is God lighting the way to Jesus' coming and His coming again.
- God is providentially involved in everything, bringing His purposes to pass.
- Because of God's providence and power, we can surrender ourselves to Him.
- The virgin birth prepares us for Jesus' extraordinary identity and ministry.
- Faith looks back to what God has done to look forward without fear.
- Born in the "House of Bread," Jesus is our "Bread of Life."
- If we are too busy, we will not make room for Jesus who has come to us.
- True worship exalts the worth of Jesus, our reigning King.
- God makes Himself known so that He may be found by all who seek Him.
- Jesus is our Passover Lamb, born to die for the sins of the world.
- Those who journey to Jesus come away changed by Him.
- The perfect gift of Jesus isn't earned but received freely by grace.
- We express our joy in Jesus by sharing Him with others.
- Glad at Jesus' arrival, we now wait with anticipation for His return.
- Jesus is good news for everyone, and so we tell the world about Him.
- The fullness of our joy is found in Jesus.
- Heavenly wisdom can't be found on earth but only in Jesus.

- Nothing is impossible through God who is mighty for you.
- God is a good Father who loves His children completely.
- Jesus secures for us upward, inward, and outward peace as we trust Him.
- The proof of God's love for you is found in Jesus who gave Himself for you.
- God limited Himself to live among us to bring us close to God.
- Jesus saves us from our past, through our present, and for a future with Himself.
- We welcome Jesus into our life with humility and worship.
- If you have Jesus, you have the greatest treasure of all.
- When Jesus is your King, you serve Him as a Kingdom citizen.
- The world will continue at war with God until Jesus defeats Satan in the end once and for all.
- God rescued His Son so that His Son might rescue everyone.
- Hallelujah! Jesus will come again!

As you think about these lessons, take some practical steps to discover, rediscover, and root such truths in your life:

Read the story of God's work every day. The Bible is the story of God proving Himself to His people. Read a little and ask, "What do I learn about God from this passage?"

When God shows Himself wonderful, tell Him. Laugh at coincidence and look for providence. When you see God organizing little pieces into a grand picture, smile and celebrate Him.

Share with others how you have seen God's greatness. Biblical community is such an important part of the spiritual life and we can strengthen one another by singing our own songs (like Moses) about God's wonderful deeds.

And, tell others about Jesus. He's too amazing *not* to share! Talk about His presence, His power, His promises. So much of the world has still not discovered how wonderful He is.

Very soon after I placed my faith in Jesus and began worshipping Him as my Savior, I learned a simple song that reflected so much of what I felt about who He was to me. It's not sung in churches much these days, but the words are a powerful reminder of who God is to me…to us:

*You are beautiful beyond description*
*Too marvelous for words*
*Too wonderful for comprehension*
*Like nothing ever seen or heard*
*Who can grasp Your infinite wisdom?*
*Who can fathom the depth of Your love?*
*You are beautiful beyond description*
*Majesty enthroned above*

*And I stand, I stand in awe of You*
*I stand, I stand in awe of You*
*Holy God to whom all praise is due*
*I stand in awe of You*

"The larger the island of knowledge, the longer the shoreline of wonder."

—Ralph W. Sockman

The mission of Central Bible Church is "Making God known by making disciples who are changed by God to change their world." We are a Kingdom-minded church committed to training leaders and laypeople through the surrender of all our resources. Your purchase of this book provides spiritual growth resources like this to others who are unable to afford them. If you believe this book would encourage your spiritual walk, but cannot afford it, we will gladly give you a copy.

To request discounts on bulk copies or to make a contribution to our local and global leadership training, please contact us:

centralpress@wearecentral.org

Learn more about the ministry of Central Bible Church online at www.wearecentral.org.

**Central Bible Church**
8001 Anderson Boulevard
Fort Worth, Texas 76120
817-274-1315

Made in the USA
Columbia, SC
26 November 2024

47514609R00093